Introduction to

Painting and Drawing

Introduction to Painting and Drawing

Edited by
John Henn

Eagle Editions

A QUANTUM BOOK

Published by Eagle Editions Ltd.
11 Heathfield
Royston
Hertfordshire SG8 5BW

This edition printed 2002

ISBN 1-86160-552-8

QUMIPD

This book is produced by
Quantum Publishing Ltd
6 Blundell Street
London N7 9BH

Printed in Singapore by
Star Standard Industries (Pte) Ltd.

CONTENTS

INTRODUCTION

IN the town where I live a road-safety poster recently appeared on the hoardings, proclaiming the message, 'Use Your Eyes Before Crossing The Road'. It is clearly intended to caution us to look more intently for impending danger from passing vehicles. And yet, this is essentially the same advice I would want to give to anyone who is thinking of learning to draw and paint – *use your eyes.* Learn to look more intently – not just when crossing a road, but in your own immediate surroundings, in a landscape, in towns and cities, in street markets and railway stations. Learn to register what you see; do more than just glance casually at the things around you.

Many beginners mistakenly believe that achieving success as an artist is somehow dependent on being able to unlock the mysterious secrets of technique alone. Techniques *are* important – and much of this book is devoted to the way that we can use various media to interpret things in different ways. But techniques are useful only in as much as they help us to organize things in such a way that we are able to say something about a particular object, or about a landscape view. But no matter how accomplished we may become, as say, with watercolours or with any other medium, unless we are able to use techniques to serve ideas – to convey our feelings about something – time spent developing technical expertise is wasted.

Anyone who has witnessed a live performance by a great actor – Laurence Olivier, John Gielguid or Paul Schofield, for instance – will be impressed not by any apparent command of acting technique, but by the fact that one is totally unaware that any technique is being employed at all. This is because great actors become the characters they portray in such a way that one is able to accept the conviction of their performance. We get the same feeling, too, when we look at drawings and paintings by Rembrandt or Degas – we are impressed by the quality of their vision, rather than by their command of technique. The painter, W. R. Sickert, once said that a drawing will tell you what a man's eyesight is worth, and it is true that by looking at a drawing we are able to understand how much an artist has uncovered about the subject he has chosen to draw. The main purpose of this book is to help the student to build up a vocabulary of techniques, so that he will gain the confidence to approach a wider range of subjects and to use techniques which are appropriate to the choice of subject. For no matter how good an idea might seem in our imagination, unless we are able to put things on to paper or canvas, we will be unable to share our vision with others. Even the most experienced artist finds that the images he actually puts down are several times removed from those first imagined or visualized. Techniques, then, help us to translate ideas into a form that is acceptable both to ourselves and to others.

All the arts are dependent on the acquisition of certain skills. The writer must understand grammar, punctuation and syntax before he can begin to deal with narrative; musicians must understand musical theory and notation before writing a score; and the artist has to concern himself with composition, colour, proportion and light and shade. This may seem off-putting to anyone who imagines that all that is necessary is to set up a canvas on an easel in a field and start squeezing out the colour from tubes of paint! It may well be satisfying to work directly in this way, but unless you know what you are doing, there is a danger that you will be so busy 'expressing' yourself that you are no longer actually looking at the subject!

One of the facts of life that most beginners must recognize is that their first efforts are unlikely to end up tastefully framed and exhibited on a gallery wall. Initially it is necessary to be concerned with the work in hand, not with any eventual display or appraisal. It is far better to work without any self-imposed pressure to produce something that is saleable, or that might be exhibited. One should try to think of learning to draw and paint as a continuing process – as a lifelong journey of discovery. Begin simply. How often have you heard someone say, 'I'd like to draw, but I don't know how to get started'? Starting is the most difficult part – and a good way of overcoming this fear is to begin by drawing a simple frame on a sheet of paper. Then, if you are drawing a still-life, say, or a view from a window, you will have to decide how you will select and dispose objects that you wish to draw in the frame. Alternatively, you might cover a sheet of white paper with a layer of tone as a base for your drawing. Try not to be afraid of the materials you draw with; treat them sometimes with respect, sometimes with contempt, but above all manipulate them so that they meet your intentions.

All forms of drawing and painting are illusory: the artist looks at objects, people and places in three dimensions and then attempts to represent them on the two-dimensional surface of a sheet of paper or canvas. To do this satisfactorily he

Above: The traditional view of the artist at his easel with palette and brushes.

Right: The Pond: L. S. Lowry. In this composition, the space is defined by the careful disposition of factory chimneys. The overall graduated hues of grey make the rows of red brick houses conspicuous. There is a strong underlying sense of design in the painting, which lends emphasis to the sense of desolation in the industrial landscape.

must learn how to use perspective to suggest depth and recession, light and shade to suggest volume and solidity, colour to evoke mood and atmosphere, contour lines to render structure and movement, and so on. But before doing any of these things he must get into the habit of becoming more observant – weak drawings usually arise from careless or hasty observation, not from the way a pencil or brush happened to be held. The best way to make progress is to learn to co-ordinate hand and eye so that your drawings and paintings bear the imprint of your visual awareness.

Try not to be too concerned with style, however tempting it might be to follow current fashion. If you concentrate on trying to draw directly from observation, your own personal 'handwriting' will gradually reveal itself. You can try to produce drawings and paintings which correspond to your own ideas of what 'art' should be like, or you can allow yourself to be governed by what you actually *see*. The first approach ends in stalemate. The second can lead to genuine discovery. In a world where there are so many distractions, perhaps the hardest thing of all is to learn how to concentrate for any length of time. Drawing and painting from direct observation, with total concentration, even for one hour can be quite exhausting. At the same time, nothing is more rewarding than the moment when one recognizes for oneself that real progress is being made.

CHOOSING A SUBJECT

THE visionary painter, Samuel Palmer, was once advised by his friend, Calvert: 'Only paint what you *love* in what you see.' It is often helpful to choose subjects which you really care about – people and places you feel close to, a particular landscape scene, objects to which you have personal, perhaps even sentimental attachments. But although there are good reasons for wanting to represent the things that interest and fascinate you most, it is also important to develop a visual curiosity about things which are less familiar; drawing and painting are means of discovering the world we inhabit.

There is no such thing as a 'suitable' subject for painting. Everything which arrests our attention is a potential subject. Yet there are undoubtedly some subjects which appeal more strongly than others. Painters, writers, and even musicians, are sometimes identified with a particular place or region of the country in which they live. Landscape painters, especially, tend to identify themselves with a place they know well. The colour of the soil, animal and plant life, the architecture, and the physical features of the land all have a bearing on the motives behind the choice of subject. Some artists prefer the immediate surroundings of the town or village where they lived since childhood – L. S. Lowry, for instance, was content with the suburban mill towns of his native Manchester. The primi-

Left: La Montagne Sainte-Victoire (1905): Paul Cézanne.
The mountain is Cézanne's best known motif; his work is closely identified with the landscape near Aix-en-Provence. By using patches of colour overlaid near the contours, he creates a sense of movement, and at the same time makes us aware of the separate planes which link one part of the composition to another.

tive painter, Alfred Wallis, found inspiration in the small fishing harbours of Cornwall. Much depends on the kind of place you happen to live in. You may not gain inspiration from your immediate surroundings, perhaps preferring a stronger light or a warmer climate. The familiarity of a place can dull the senses; it often happens, for example, that students who leave home to study in another part of the world, rediscover the seemingly hidden features of their homeland when they return a few years later. Quite often the choice of location represents an escape from everyday routine. An artist living in Sheffield, for instance, might be tempted to wander towards the nearby Derbyshire Dales to paint the rugged escarpment of the limestone outcrops. Conversely, an artist living in a small village might be moved by the steelworks and industrial landscape of Sheffield. Industrial landscapes are often more interesting compositionally than rural ones.

This raises the whole question of what we call the 'picturesque' in drawing and painting. There are many romantic subjects which have occupied artists for generations. A visit to any local art exhibition of the many groups and art societies up and down the country will reveal a similarity in the choice of subjects: rustic barns in a cornfield feathered with poppies, dramatic mountain scenes, fishing boats winched up on the foreshore, country churches in riverside settings, and so on. If one is to avoid these clichés, one must look to find new relationships in the most ordinary circumstances, to try to make new discoveries even in the most familiar subjects. Most of all make sure that you have something to say about the subject you have selected.

Still-life as a subject makes a useful introduction to all the problems that one might encounter later on in dealing with landscape and figure studies. It has, also, one distinct advantage: inanimate objects can be placed in position for as long as required, under the same lighting conditions. Of course, if the painting goes on a long time, flowers and fruit may deteriorate; but usually there should be more than enough time to get to grips with the subject. Forget about candlesticks and chianti bottles, and any other preconceived ideas you may have about what a still-life group should look like. With a little imagination you should be able to select and arrange objects in such a way that the resulting drawing or painting will reflect your own interests and visual judgement. Giorgio Morandi, for example, painted hundreds of still-life paintings, using the same mundane artefacts, arranged in different ways, against variously coloured backgrounds and under varying conditions of light.

Figure-drawing can be done in the academic setting of a formal drawing class or in the informal setting of your own home. Friends and relatives are often willing to sit for an hour or so, and young children can sometimes be persuaded to pose for shorter periods of time. Sketchbooks can be used for rapid notations of figures in movement, or in crowded streets. Small pocket sketchbooks are best for making drawings inconspicuously on train or boat journeys.

Above left: Smaller sketchbooks are useful for working in confined areas; when travelling by train for instance, or, in a market place.

Above right: Cartridge pads can be used for working rapidly in a variety of media, including, pencil, pen & ink, and watercolour.

Landscape is undoubtedly the most popular subject for both amateur and professional painters alike. Yet it is also, in my view, the most difficult to handle. Landscape is indeterminate, and one needs a strong sense of composition, sharp visual judgement and a sure feeling for atmosphere to be able to select and render the diverse elements in a landscape which are disposed at various levels receding into distance. But, of course, nothing is more enjoyable than to be in the open air on a fine day with paints and a sketchbook! Industrial cities, towns and crowded interiors are subjects worth more consideration. Think also about drawing people engaged in specific occupations – in hospitals, railway stations, sports centres and so on. There are many subjects which beckon our attention; it is left to us to decide which subjects move us sufficiently to want to say something about them.

Colour

It is a mistake, in my view, to think of colour as a separate component of drawing and painting. Understanding colour is an integral part of the whole business of learning to see and learning to register what you see. A basic knowledge of colour theory is, of course, useful, but time spent observing colour in nature is even more rewarding. Cézanne said that painting from direct observation is a way of classifying one's sensations of colour. 'Drawing and colour,' he added, 'are not separate at all; in so far as you paint you draw. The more the colour harmonizes, the more exact the drawing becomes.'

Contemporary colour theory is founded upon the experiments of Sir Isaac Newton (1642–1727). Newton explained that although sunlight, or white light, is 'uncoloured', it is made up of seven coloured rays: violet, indigo, blue, green, yellow, orange and red. We see colour in objects that reflect and absorb these rays to a greater or lesser degree. The terracotta roof of a house in Spain, for example, is a warm, dark-red colour at first light, when the sun is low. At midday, however, when the sun is directly overhead, that same roof becomes a pink-orange white. Colour theory often gets in the way of how we actually see colour – one needs to be able to see beyond the 'local' colour of objects. The 'local' colour of an olive tree, for instance, might be green or grey-green; but under strong sunlight the leaves might sparkle like silvered viridian and at dusk become shadowy-black silhouettes. So we need to observe carefully how the effect of light can modify our preconception of the colour that an object should be.

An object which reflects all the coloured rays of the spectrum appears as white light; an object that absorbs them all appears black. When we talk of light being 'absorbed', we are really saying that it is lost. When rays of light are not absorbed, by an object such as a flint wall, for instance, they are reflected in the direction from which they came. The term 'refracted' light refers to the phenom-

Below: 'White light', or uncoloured light, is made up of the seven colours of the spectrum. The colours are separated when filtered through a prism.

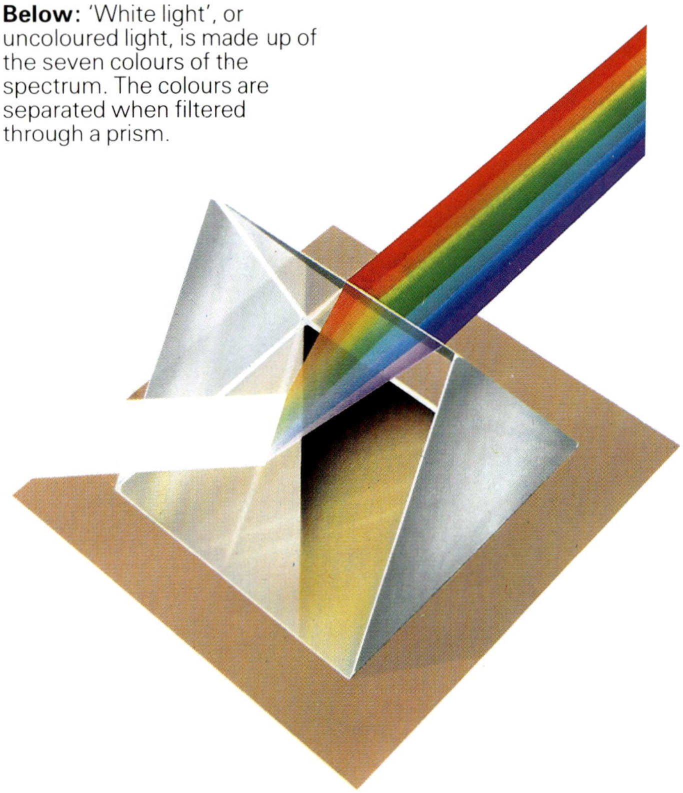

Above: *Colour wheel:* The inner wheels represent the effect of combining primary colours in the outer wheels.

enon of light passing through a transparent, or partly transparent, body: the light is redirected, or 'refracted'.

We must realize, therefore, that colour is modified by light. It often happens, for example, that travelling along a country lane, we see a scene which arouses our interest. Returning with sketchbook and paints a few days later, how disappointing it is to find that same scene transformed, no longer as interesting as it was before. What happens is that our attention is drawn by the way that things appear under certain conditions of light at a particular time of day. We forget that appearances are continually changing – especially in a northern climate.

An artist's palette must necessarily be selected from the range of colours available. We need to discover, then, how to express our sensations of colour by mixing colours together. The colours produced by mixing can only be an approximation of the transitory effects of light on the colours we see around us. We use colour to describe the things we see and to do this effectively we need to be aware of the power of contrast – colours in the light are equivalent to the colours in shadow. We can also use colour to make things appear to advance or recede.

Colours can be divided into two categories, warm and cool. An excellent exercise for any painter is to mix a range of greys which are cool (blue-greys) and also a range of warm greys (red-greys). The range should be quite extensive. Then proceed to paint your subject – still-life, landscape or whatever – using this range of colours only. In this way you will learn very effectively how to work without relying on primary colours or strong contrasts.

The three primary colours are red, yellow and blue; all other colours are formed from the primaries. The three secondary colours are made from the mixture of two primaries; they are green (blue and yellow), violet (red and blue) and orange (yellow and red). The shade of a secondary colour varies according to the proportions in which the two primary colours are mixed together. Green, for instance, can tend towards blue or yellow. Complementary colours are those colours which can be paired on the colour circle – red is the complement of green, yellow of blue, and so on.

PERSPECTIVE

WHEN we look across a valley from a high vantage-point, we see all the elements in nature that make up a landscape, arranged at varying distances from each other. Trees in the foreground, middle-distance and far-distance are perhaps linked by paths, hedgerows and rivers. To draw these things 'in perspective' means only that we

Above: Additive primaries
Red, green and blue are called additive primaries because white light results from combining them. A third colour is produced when any two additive primaries are combined.

Above: Subtractive primaries
The colours produced by combining two additive primaries are called subtractive primaries. Cyan for example, is made by mixing blue and green. When white light is filtered through three subtractive primaries, black is produced.

Left: *Colour tree:* Colours are divided into different hues. The amount of white or black contained in each colour determines its hue. The tree illustrates only the main variations.

need to find a way of representing the distance of one object from another – in other words, 'fixing' their position in our drawing.

There are certain ground-rules which act as a useful guide in doing this, but as with all art theory, there is no real substitute for training the hand and eye to register things directly without recourse to drawing systems.

The picture plane is a kind of imaginary vertical screen, which is transparent and which is positioned on the ground at a distance from the artist, depending on where he intends his drawing to begin. The 'picture' he conceives lies behind this imaginary screen, although some objects in the immediate foreground would touch it. The precise position of the viewer on his side of the picture plane is critical. This will determine how high the eye is from ground level and whether he is in the centre or to one side of the picture. The base of the picture plane is called the ground line. It is from the ground line that one's measurements begin.

The artist stands on one side of the picture plane, and on the other side all the things that can be seen are disposed at various points towards the horizon. The horizon line is parallel to the ground line and is the same height as the eye of the viewer. On the horizon line is a point we call the 'vanishing' point. This may be in the centre, or to one side, depending on the position of the viewer.

When the vanishing point has been established as the horizon line, then all vertical lines remain vertical and all lines which are parallel to the ground line remain parallel. Imagine, for instance, that you are standing immediately facing the side of a tall building. Then neither the vertical or horizontal lines will converge. For them to do so it is necessary to move backwards, or to one side.

The lines other than those which are vertical or parallel to the ground line are drawn towards the vanishing point. In a landscape, for example, objects of roughly the same size – trees or telegraph poles – appear to become smaller as they recede into the distance, and as they get smaller they seem to be nearer the horizon line. Although they diminish in size, there is no distortion in their shapes when seen from the front.

In the accompanying diagram you will notice that the tree in the foreground coincides with the picture plane and the size remains constant. One can therefore find the actual height or width of any object by assessing it in relation to the ground line. On the other hand, the size of an object as it appears in perspective can be determined by taking a line from the ground line to the vanishing point. All the horizontal lines which appear at right angles to the picture plane will converge on the horizon at the

Right: One point perspective
As the parallel lines recede, they appear to converge at the vanishing point. If only two sides of the cube are visible, it can be drawn in perspective from a single vanishing point.

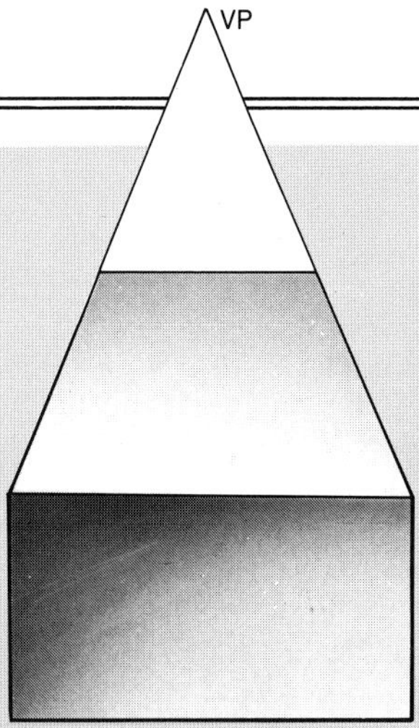

Right: Two point perspective
When three sides of the cube are visible, two sets of parallel lines converge at separate vanishing points.

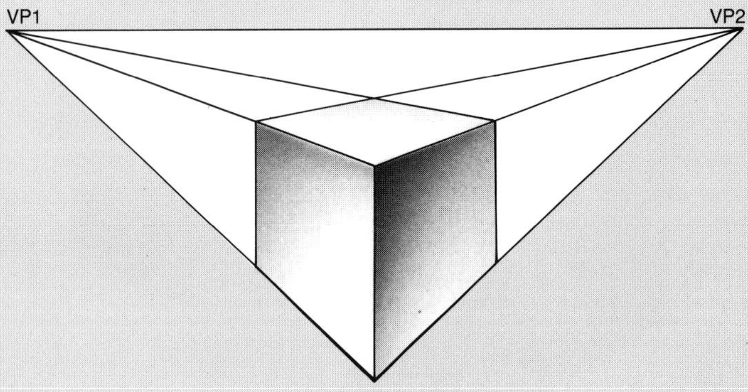

Right: Three point perspective
When the cube appears either above or below the artist's view of the horizon, it is necessary to draw both vertical and horizontal lines converging on three separate vanishing points.

Right: The horizon line is placed at sea level. You can try this out standing on a beach by holding a ruler up at eye-level. In a more undulating landscape, the horizon line will probably be partially concealed, but it can still be established in the drawing.

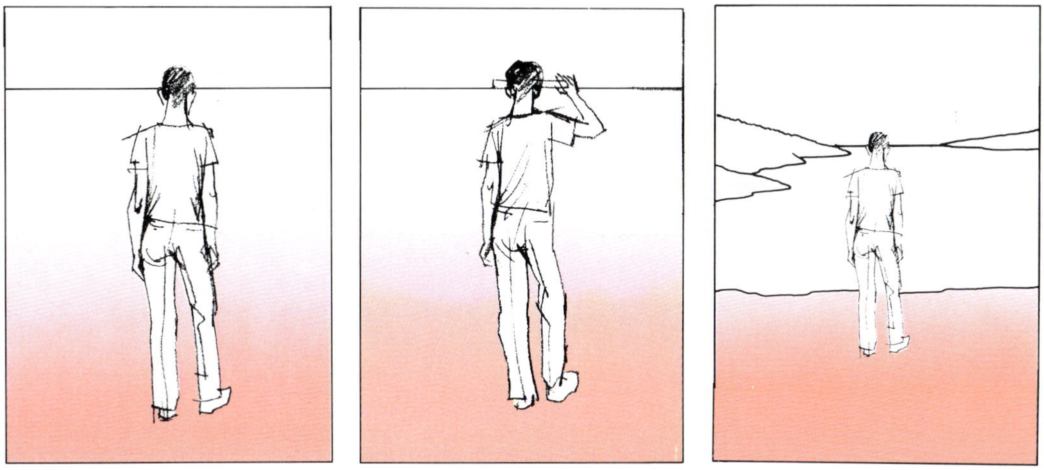

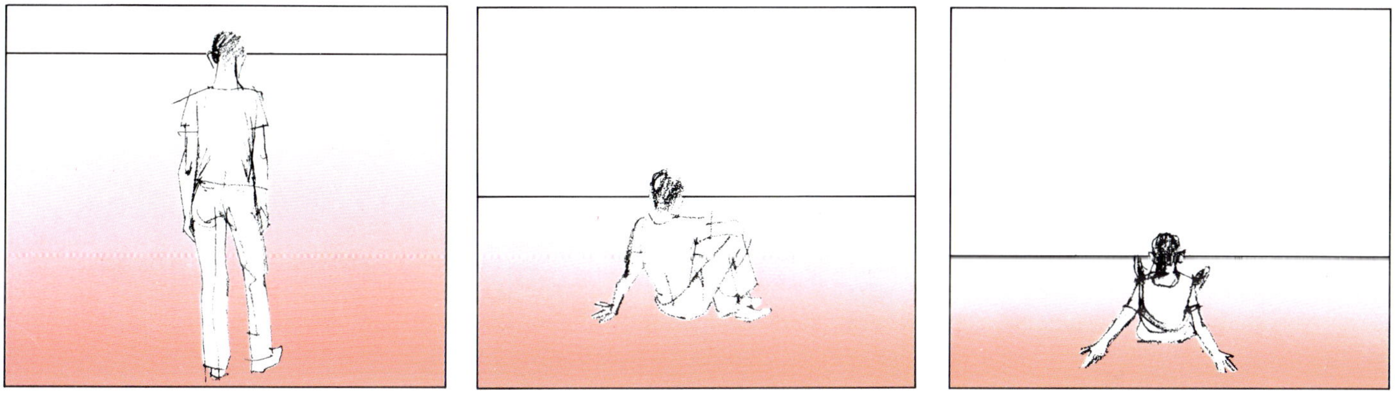

vanishing point. If you were drawing a box placed in the centre of your line of vision, there would be one vanishing point. If, however, you were to draw two separate boxes several metres distant from each other, there would be two sets of parallel lines, each set with its own vanishing point. Strong diagonal lines which incline steeply upwards have their vanishing point above the horizon; conversely, those inclining sharply downwards have their vanishing point below the horizon line.

Above: These three illustrations show how the horizon line changes according to the way you position your body. In a standing position for instance, most of the ground plane is visible. But the subject itself should suggest the best eye-level for your drawing.

Below: The picture plane is an imaginary transparent screen separating the artist from the subject. The image that you see through this plane is what is transferred to your paper or canvas. When starting to draw, the horizon line should be established first.

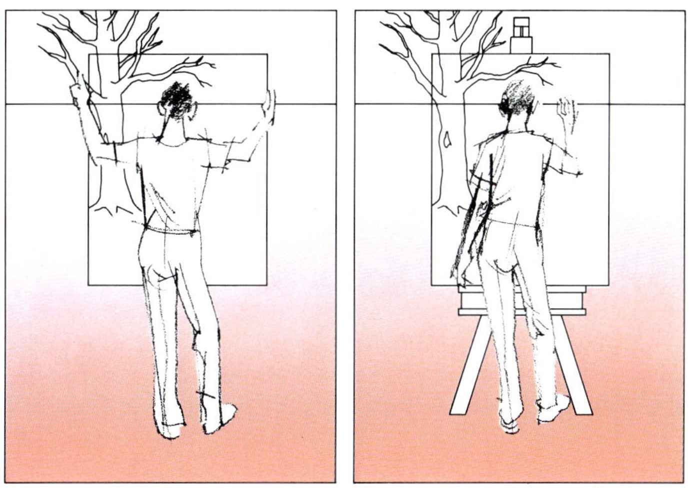

COMPOSITION

WHEN an artist produces a painting from visual notes (sketchbook studies made from direct observation) he is putting together, or 'composing', a pictorial statement. It is this act of putting things together, satisfactorily, that makes a well-composed painting.

Every time an artist produces a drawing or painting – a portrait, figure study, landscape, still-life, or whatever subject is in view – he is consciously or unconsciously, composing. There are painters whose work follows very

Left: Beach at Trouville: Claude Monet (1840–1926) This painting has a strong sense of design; the characteristic shape of the umbrellas serves to provide a link from one side of the composition to the other. Monet's sense of visual judgement was so acute, that he was able to place the elements in his compositions intuitively, rather than by relying on mathematical formulae. The placement of the chair roughly relates to the golden section, and prevents the composition becoming too symmetrical.

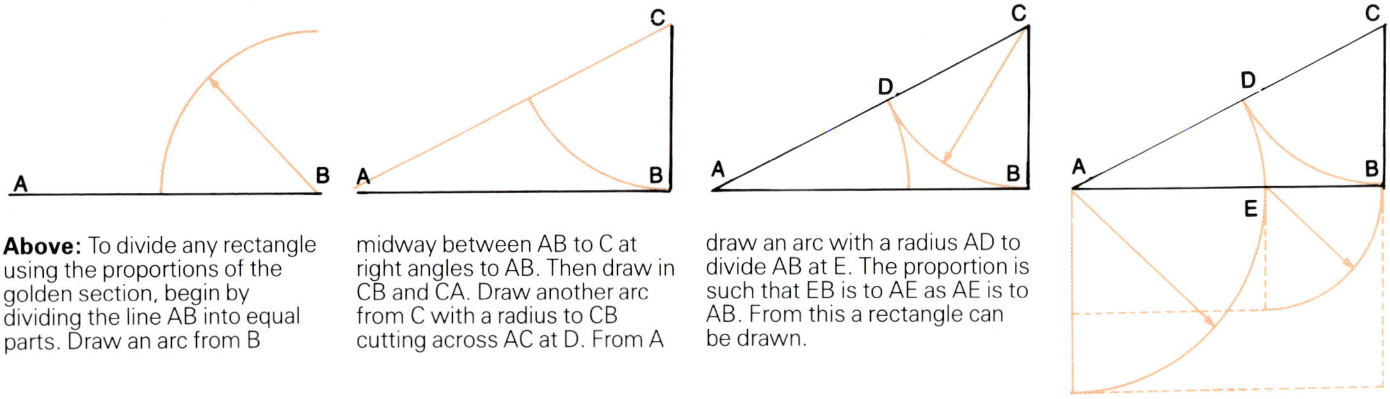

Above: To divide any rectangle using the proportions of the golden section, begin by dividing the line AB into equal parts. Draw an arc from B midway between AB to C at right angles to AB. Then draw in CB and CA. Draw another arc from C with a radius to CB cutting across AC at D. From A draw an arc with a radius AD to divide AB at E. The proportion is such that EB is to AE as AE is to AB. From this a rectangle can be drawn.

closely the classical rules of composition, and others who work more intuitively. One is more conscious of formal composition in a Degas pastel, say, than in an oil painting by Bonnard. Much depends on what the artist is trying to say – studies of the ballet, with groups of dancers on stage, require considered placement in the composition. A casual glimpse of some domestic scene can be less formal.

In the pastel, *Woman at her toilet*, by Degas, for example, there is an interesting relationship between all the component parts of the drawing; nothing is wasted in the drawing and everything connects. The accent is on the strong diagonal movement of the arm brushing the hair and the edge of the table. The tall pot on the extreme right of the composition is the one important vertical shape and helps restore balance. The arms of the girl brushing her hair have a firm rhythmic link with the arms of the standing figure whose head is cropped by the top edge of the picture. But the main emphasis lies in the broad brushstrokes used to delineate the figure and related objects.

A painting can be placed historically by its compositional values. Early religious paintings were usually composed symmetrically to support rich decoration and pattern. Renaissance painters discovered a new feeling for space, created by the introduction of perspective. Classical modes of composition reached near-perfection in the work of Poussin and Claude. The French Impressionists adopted a more random approach to composition inspired by snapshot photography.

The way that a picture is composed will largely be determined by the subject. Landscape is indeterminate and requires a firm organization to make the various parts of the composition jell. Selection and visual judgement are critical, since one can deal with only a comparatively small area of the total scene in view. With a still-life painter, on the other hand, one can physically pick up and arrange each component, so that the process of composing begins before one starts to draw.

The classical concept of composition is based on the logical arrangement of pictorial elements. Line, shape and colour are organized in such a way that they work together in the design as a whole. Underlying all the work of classically composed painting is a firm linear structure, which is sometimes simple, sometimes complex. No matter how rich and varied the surface qualities of the painting are, everything is held together by the linear structure of the composition. This structure is sometimes called the painter's 'secret' geometry, because the final painting usually conceals much of the underlying drawing. Some painters – Degas is one of them – allow us to see the process of their compositional ideas, by a skilful interaction between the linear and surface aspects of their paintings.

The division of space known as the Golden Section is perhaps the best known system of proportion in pictorial composition. The simplest method of finding the Golden Section in any given rectangle is to take a sheet of paper of the size one is working to and fold it in half three times in succession (do this for both the length and breadth of the paper). The folds will divide the paper into eight equal parts, from which a 3:5 ratio can be determined. (Alternative ratios might be 2:3, 5:8 or 8:13.) In the work of artists such as Piero della Francesca, the vertical division of the Golden Section is used to determine the placement of the central figure of Christ. Similarly, in the work of other painters, it is used to place the most important element in the composition. As we develop our powers of observation, however, we sometimes unconsciously place the most significant vertical element in our drawing on that same division in the painting. In landscape the horizon presents a natural division of the total area of the painting. In lowland areas, where the sky is dominant, the horizon will be quite low, as in the work of Rembrandt and other Dutch painters. Where there are hills and mountains, the horizon might be placed high in the composition to give emphasis to rising forms.

There are certain compositional conventions which appear time and time again in 'picturesque' paintings: rivers and paths which lead the eye from foreground to significant objects in the distance; trees with masses of

Left and far left: The compositions of Piero della Francesca (c.1420–92) are usually founded upon an intricate mathematical division of space. In his 'Baptism of Christ', the verticals of the figures and trees harmonise with the implied circle which has a dove at its centre. At the same time, the stream in the foreground leads the eye into the heart of the landscape.

Right: Coming from evening church: Samuel Palmer
This simply-composed painting of a procession of figures from the church to a woodland path, is strongly symbolic. The arched branches of the trees create a vignette, the moon and church steeple provide visual equivalents to the figures in the foreground. By using closely painted tones, Palmer was able to evoke a sense of mood and atmosphere.

Opposite: Still-life with water jug: Paul Cézanne.
Even when left unfinished, Cézanne's paintings and drawings have a completeness about them – every brush mark serves a purpose. Cézanne allowed the white ground of the canvas to form an integral part of the total composition. The artist also took great care in the actual placement of the objects before he began painting a still-life.

foliage on one side with glimpses of the distant horizon bathed in sunlight; and so on. When one is producing a landscape painting from direct observation one has the advantage of being able to leave out anything one might consider excessive to the composition as a whole. And it is this fact which distinguishes the work of the beginner from the more experienced painter. When we first start to draw from direct observation, we put everything in, but with experience we learn to be more selective – to imply, rather than overstate.

Tonal contrast plays an important part in composition. The balance of light and dark shapes connects the various parts of a drawing or painting. One might begin by using just three or four tones from light to dark. Don't be confused by colour and tone; if we look at a black and white photograph of a colourful painting, the tones representing each colour allow us to 'read' the image, because we are able to distinguish the light and dark shapes. A painting

can often fail because of a lack of tonal unity. Some painters solve this problem by using colour almost monochromatically. In the pastoral paintings of Samuel Palmer, for instance, there are gradations of yellow ochres to dark sombre browns from which the whites glow.

Composition is not concerned simply with static shapes. Rhythm and movement are the life of a painting. Even seemingly static subjects, such as seascapes and portraits, are dependent on a sense of movement. For even though a figure may be sitting perfectly still, a drawing or painting should suggest that the sitter is capable of movement. The still-life by Paul Cézanne, for example, is full of interlocking rhythms which make the painting anything but 'still'. His use of complementary colours gives the contours of the drawing a vibrancy.

It is in the work of Van Gogh, however, that one becomes acutely aware of the disturbing conflicting rhythms that reveal the artist's personality.

CHAPTER 1

MEDIA & MATERIALS

MEDIA/MATERIALS

THE artist today commands a tremendous range of materials and potential work methods – so much so that at times one can become bewildered by the choice available. In the beginning one should be open to all the possibilities, but at the same time cautious of seeking solutions through media alone. After a number of years it usually happens that one develops a preference for one medium or another, for certain supports to paint on, drawing materials and techniques. The French illustrator, André François, is said to have produced some of his most memorable pen drawings with pens that he could find only in French post offices!

The preparation of materials is in itself a craft. Too much time spent on preparation can only delay the moment when one actually confronts one's subject. Most contemporary artists, therefore, prefer to purchase their materials ready for use. Even egg-tempera paint can now be bought ready-prepared in tubes.

There are two essential points to bear in mind when considering the choice of medium – first, the inherent qualities of the medium and, second, its suitability for the subject to be painted. If, for example, one is attempting to express the fleeting qualities of light in a landscape, then watercolour might be more suitable than oil or pastel. If, on the other hand, one wishes to evoke the particular colour relationships in a costume figure drawing, then pastel might be more appropriate.

A brush, pencil, pen, chalk or piece of charcoal – each makes its individual mark. There is no point in trying to make a piece of charcoal produce the same kind of detail that can be more readily obtained with a pencil or pen. So we should begin by asking ourselves a number of questions before starting to draw or paint. Suppose we are about to begin a figure study for a standing pose to last fifteen minutes. The model puts all his weight on one leg. We want to express that sense of weight bearing downwards through the body to the floor. Given the time available and the pose, charcoal might be the most suitable medium to render the main proportions rapidly and to give emphasis to the solidity of the figure with strong contour lines.

When artists describe their work, they sometimes talk about struggling with a technique. It seems that a medium that offers some resistance to the artist – oil or pastels, for instance – enables him continually to change and readjust things so that images are made and developed until a satisfactory result is achieved.

SUPPORTS

WATERCOLOUR

THE luminous character of watercolour is dependent on a suitable paper support. Paper of good quality is important; inexpensive papers, such as machine-made cartridge paper, do not hold the washes very well. Essentially there are three different types of paper surfaces which are used for watercolour – hot-pressed (HP), cold-pressed (CP), also known as 'not', and rough.

Cold-pressed papers tend to be used more frequently than the others. Hot-pressed papers are used more for combined techniques, such as pen and wash, or for combining gouache with watercolour. Rough-textured papers are attractive to handle, but the pronounced tooth is unsuitable for delicate or detailed brushwork. There are numerous handmade papers, many of which have a toned surface such as 'De Wint'. The maker's name appears as a watermark and should be read the right way round to denote the right side to work on. Watercolour papers are selected by weight as well as for their surface qualities. The weight is measured by the ream (480 sheets). An average weight for a sheet size A2 would be 90lb. Stretching dampened paper with gummed tape is necessary only with the lighter weights of paper. English papers include R.W.S. (Royal Watercolour Society), Saunders, Bockingford and Crisbrook. French, Italian and Dutch papers are also widely available. Papers such as Arches (French) and Fabriano (Italian) are best purchased in large rolls which are less expensive. They can be cut into smaller sheets.

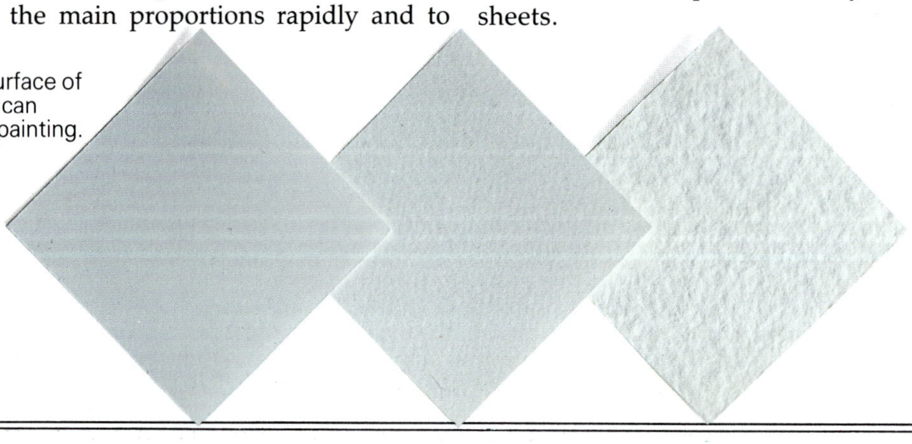

Right: The textured surface of the watercolour paper can influence the finished painting.

Above: There is a wide variety of white and toned watercolour papers available to the artist. The tone of the paper however should not be too dark, since the transparent glazes of watercolour would be lost.

Above right and right: Handmade papers are delightful to work on – the right side of the paper is determined by reading the manufacturer's watermark in the right direction. Where no watermark is used, the right side is that which has been coated with size.

OIL/ACRYLICS/TEMPERA

Stretched canvas is the most common support for oil painting. A variety of cloth can be adapted for use, but linen is considered to be the most suitable. Coarse and fine weaves of linen are equally attractive – the coarse weaves being used generally for very large canvases. Cotton can be bought ready primed for use. Wood panels are suitable so long as the wood is of sufficient thickness to avoid warping or buckling. The wood should also be well-seasoned and not kiln-dried. Hardboard, or masonite, is inexpensive and easy to handle and prepare; it is undoubtedly the most popular support used by students and beginners. The *smooth* side, *not* the textured side, should be used. Sandpaper the surface with a medium grade of sandpaper before priming. Cardboard and binder's millboard are ideal supports for oil painting and acrylics, though the paint must be applied fairly thinly. Plywood is light and, if primed with a number of coats, highly suitable for painting in oil. Prepared canvas – linen or cotton – can be bought ready for stretching on to a wooden frame. Stretchers are sold with small wooden wedges which, when knocked into the slotted corners of the frame, give the canvas a final tension. The canvas is cut with an over-

Above: Firm supports for oil and tempera painting: Although canvas is still the most widely used support for oil painting, wood can also be used including: mahogany (7) hardboard (2) blockboard (3) and plywood (5). Thinner boards require additional support to prevent warping and buckling. Chipboard (4) requires no support. Heavy duty cardboard is absorbent and should be sized (6).Canvas boards can be bought ready-primed for use. metal supports are rarely used, but copper (8) is the best surface to work on. Various types of paper can be pasted to a firm support and sized (1).

Opposite: The choice of canvas texture should be determined by the type of subject to be painted – coarse canvas makes an excellent base support for strongly expressive work, whereas a fine weave canvas is more suited to detailed brushwork.

10 oz cotton duck No. 1
12 oz cotton duck No. 1
15 oz cotton duck No. 1
9 oz cotton duck No. 2
Fine linen
(embroidery linen)
Fine artists' linen
Unbleached calico
Flax
Coarse hessian
Prepared canvas

1 Check that the stretcher is square by measuring from corner to corner.

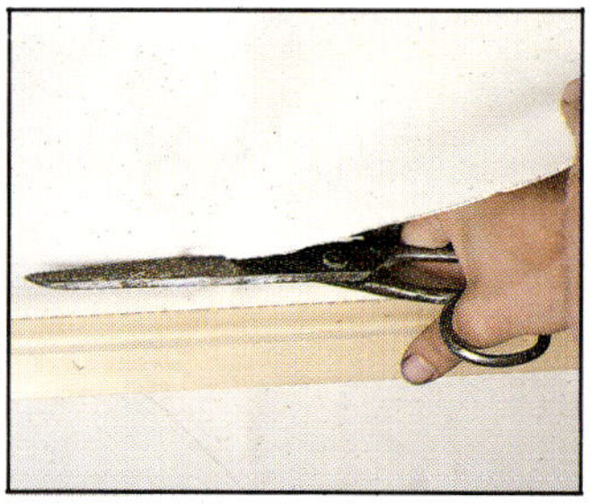

2 Place the stretcher on the canvas and cut an overlap of at least 2"/5cm on each side.

3 Fold the overlap over the stretcher and put a staple in the centre of each side while keeping the canvas taut.

4 Carefully fold the corners and secure with two or three staples so that they are neat and tidy.

5 Continue to staple at regular intervals of about 2"/5cm.

6 Gently knock in the tension pegs to make the canvas really taut on the stretcher.

1 Applying size to the canvas. The size is dissolved in hot water in a double boiler and brushed into the weave.

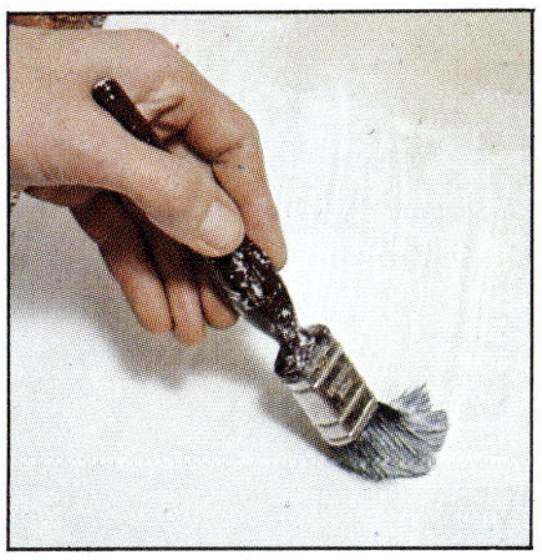

2 The white coat of primer is applied when the size is dry. It should be thinly applied in two or more coats.

lap of about 4cm. Tack or staple centrally on one side and then tension and tack from the opposite side. Continue on all sides until the canvas is evenly stretched.

The canvas is primed in two stages: first it is sized, then it is given two or three coats of primer. The sizing is usually done with a mixture of water and powdered bone – one part glue to seven parts water. The mixture is gently stirred and heated and applied to the canvas while still warm. Make sure that it soaks well into the weave. The primer is made from six parts turpentine, one part linseed oil and flake white powder. The turps and oil are blended together and added gradually to the flake white and then mixed to a cream-like consistency. Allow one coat of primer to dry thoroughly before applying another. Some artists prefer an emulsion primer made from one part whiting (flake white), one part zinc oxide, one part glue size and one-half part linseed oil. The whiting and size powder are mixed together and blended with a few drops of warm liquid size to make a paste. The linseed oil is then added drop by drop and well beaten until dissolved.

3 Staining the white ground. The paint is thinned with turpentine in a tin in sufficient quantity to cover the whole canvas.

4 The stain is brushed quickly over the entire surface.

5 The excess paint is removed with a pad of dry rag leaving the stain in the weave of the canvas.

BRUSHES

It is something of a false economy to buy cheap brushes for painting either in oil or watercolour. Good-quality sable or hog's-hair brushes will last a considerable length of time if properly cared for.

Oil-painting brushes are made from red sable or from white hog's hair. Sable brushes are generally used for glazes and for working with paint that has been thinned down with turpentine and linseed oil. Hog bristles hold

Left: The main ingredients for making a primer suitable for both canvas and board.

Below: Soft sable brushes are produced in a series of sizes. The brushes illustrated are all size 5 made by different manufacturers. A number of synthetic sable brushes are available and though they are generally of good quality they do not retain as much water-colour in the bristle as real sable.

greater quantities of paint and are ideal for achieving an impasto texture. New hog's-hair brushes should be soaked in warm water for 24 hours to soften the bristles. There are three main shapes of brush – 'round', 'filbert' and 'bright'. Brights are short-bristled with a chisel edge and are used for covering large areas with varying consistencies of paint. Rounds are used for fine detail – especially in portraiture. Filberts have a slightly curved edge and are useful for broadly-drawn contours in the preliminary brushwork for landscapes and figure studies. All three types of brush are produced in a range of sizes from one to 12 or even larger. In recent years considerable improvements have been made to synthetic brushes, but even the best lack the 'bite' of genuine sable or hog's hair.

Some artists prefer to work with flexible palette knives rather than brushes, especially when laying on broad areas of undiluted paint. Watercolour brushes are expensive, but there is no real substitute for fine-quality sable. Squirrel and ox-hair brushes, which are less expensive, can be used to complete the range of sizes available. For drawing with a brush a No. 3 or No. 4 red sable is ideal; squirrel and ox-hair brushes can be used for laying on broader washes of colour. Brushes should be washed

Left: Flexible palette knives were originally used solely for colour mixing. They can be used instead of a brush, as a tool for laying on a thick impasto of oil or acrylic paint. Additionally, they can be used to scrape away paint when a particular passage in a painting needs to be removed.

Below: The brushes shown are *(from left to right)* mop wash goat, synthetic, mixed fibres, squirrel, ox-hair round, pony-camel, sable fan, sable bright, sable round and sable lettering.

Above and right:
The three main types of pencil used for drawing, are: clutch pencil, propelling pencil, and the traditional wooden pencil. For tonal variation graphite and carbon pencils are invaluable. Coloured wax pencils are produced in an extensive range of colours, some of which are water-soluble.

and rinsed after use, and reshaped by squeezing out surplus water with the thumb and forefinger. Soft rags and sponges may also be used to apply colour or to reduce the strength of colour washes applied too heavily.

PENCIL

FROM childhood we have used pencils to scribble, make notes and record our responses to things seen and imagined. Pencils offer the most direct, and the most versatile, means of allowing our thoughts to flow from the mind through the finger tips to a sheet of paper. The artist is concerned with varying degrees of softness to express different qualities in a drawing. There is usually a choice of twelve grades, from the pale, hard lines of a 6H to the soft, graduated tones of 6B. Most artists tend to work with a medium-soft pencil – grade 2B or 3B – and these can render most of the tones required. Harder pencils are

Above right:
Graphite pencils are graded from very hard to very soft. The hardest makes a faint fine line; the softest a dense, granular black. By drawing on different types of paper with different grades of pencil, a rich variety of textures can be achieved.

1 The graduated tone is achieved by using a 4B (soft) pencil on a smooth paper.
2 The same pencil used on a rough watercolour paper renders a totally different quality.
3 By indenting lines into the surface of the paper with the blunt rounded end of the pencil, a negative effect is produced when tone is applied.
4 Pencil erasers can be used as a drawing tool to create highlights from passages of softly drawn pencil tones.
5 Black wax pencil reveals the grain of the paper.
6 The dust scraped from a very soft pencil lead can be spread with a finger to create a soft tone.

Above: *Pencil grades*
Eight different grades of pencil were shaded across a piece of paper in varying tones to show the differences between grades. The pencils were *(top to bottom):* 10H, 7H, 3H, 2H, HB, 3B, 6B, and EE.

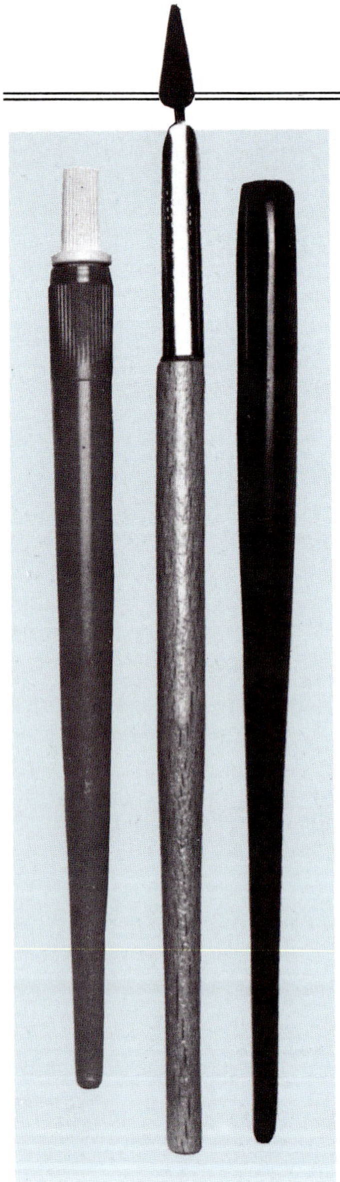

sometimes useful when trying to render structure or architectural subjects. The quality of line and tone will depend to some extent on the choice of paper used. A paper with a heightened grain such as a watercolour paper will enhance the soft grades of pencil; a hard pencil used on the same paper might be too incisive and simply tear into the surface. White cartridge is perfectly adequate for most purposes, but certain papers accept the full range of tone. Mould-made papers, such as Ingres, Fabriano or Saunders, are especially suitable.

PEN & INK

RENDERING line with pen and ink is a technique embedded in Greek, Roman and Egyptian history. Ancient documents and books were often illustrated with pen drawings. Quills were generally sharpened and dipped in ink, though reeds and bamboo shoots were also brought into use. There are some fine examples of drawings with a quill pen in the notebooks of Leonardo Da Vinci and Rembrandt used a pen very lucidly, often combining the drawn line with washes of sepia ink to give strong tonal contrasts. The modern nib is not much different from the bronze nibs made by the Romans. A great variety of pens were developed, culminating in the modern fountain variety, which houses the ink in a reservoir, usually a rubber tube inside the hollow handle of the pen.

Pen and ink is not a medium for the faint-hearted: decision-making takes place before committing pen to paper and mistakes are difficult to erase. The quality of

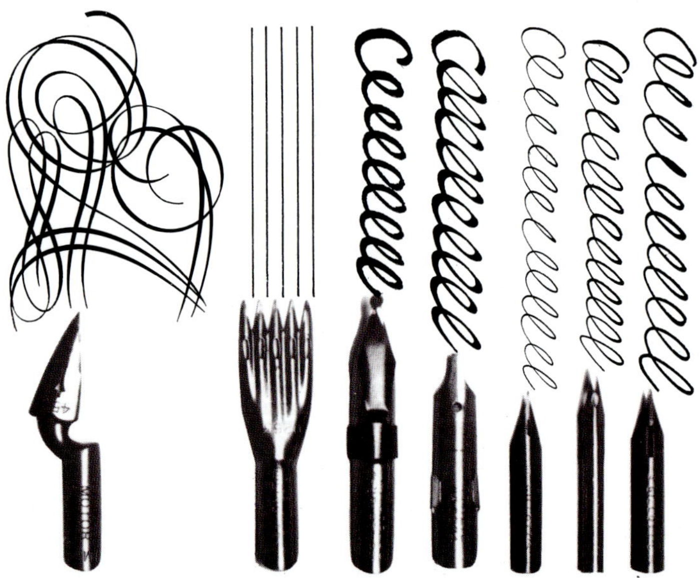

Above: *Pen Holders*
Most nibs will fit into a standard holder. For fine lines, mapping pen nibs are fitted into a smaller holder. Brass reservoirs can be attached to most holders to retain more ink.

Above: Bamboo pens and quills have very long histories, but are still made today.

Left: *Nibs and lines*
Contrasting linear qualities can be obtained by using fine, italic, thick and multiple points.

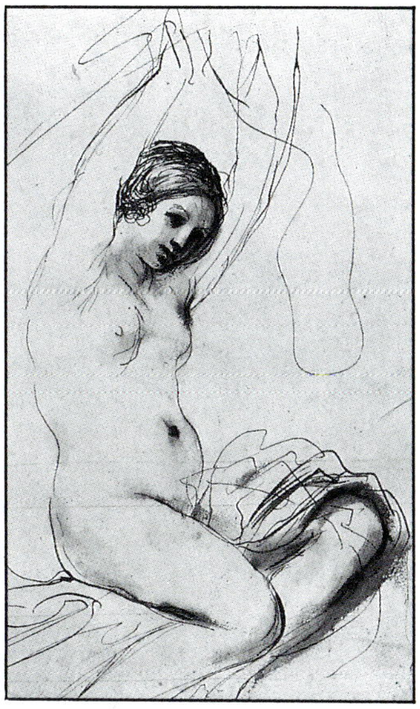

Above: Study of a woman: Guercino (Giovanni Barbieri) The free lucid line was obtained by using a fairly broad metal nib. Washes of ink were added to heighten the sense of form.

Above: View of Arles: Vincent Van Gogh. This drawing clearly demonstrates how Van Gogh was able to achieve the sense of depth and movement in his pen drawings by using thick and thin pen lines in short strokes.

line is critical to the success of the drawing. That is why the traditional nib is so much better than a mechanical drawing pen, which offers no variety in the thickness of the line. The pen drawings of Van Gogh, for instance, make use of the characteristic strokes of both nib and reed pen, with thick and thin lines used with uneven pressure. Segonzac is another artist whose work demonstrates an exquisite feeling for line.

Dip pens are inexpensive and can hold a variety of nibs from fine to broad chisel-edged shapes. Brass reservoirs can be attached to some nibs to retain more ink, but they tend to clog easily and need cleaning frequently. Fountain pens work best with non-waterproof ink, though some pens are made specifically to be used with waterproof India ink. It is well worthwhile experimenting with other drawing implements, such as the traditional quill (which can be made from pigeon feathers) or sharpened bamboo. The quality of line produced is quite different from that made by a metal nib. There are a number of dense, black drawing inks available.

Below: *Drawing inks*
The types of ink used for pen drawing include Rotring inks in plastic containers and cartridges for use in technical drawing pens, Pelikan and Quink fountain pen ink, Higgins black, and Rotring and Grumbacher black which are ideal for sketching, and a variety of coloured waterproof inks.

Below: *Types of Charcoal*
(1, 2) Compressed charcoal pencils are graded from hard to soft. Stick charcoal comes in different widths – thick **(3)** medium **(6)** and thin **(7)**. Compressed charcoal **(4)** is darker in tone and powdered charcoal **(5)** is spread with a paper torchon.

CHARCOAL

THE technique of drawing with a stick of charred wood has been in existence since man first felt the need to express himself visually. The charcoal in use today is burned in special kilns so that it is evenly charred. The wood used is willow or vine twigs. Charcoal is a particularly pleasant medium to draw with; it can be soft and yet capable of producing sharp, precise lines. The strength of line and tone can be easily modified with a finger tip, allowing contours to be constantly restated. For this reason it is an ideal medium for gaining confidence in drawing.

Originally charcoal was thought of as a means of providing an under-drawing for painting; consequently, most early charcoal drawings are buried under layers of paint. During the nineteenth century it came to be used more frequently as a medium in its own right. The French Impressionists found in charcoal an ideal medium for capturing the fleeting nuances of nature. And in his series of drawings of dancers, Degas produced some of his finest charcoal drawings.

The texture of the paper used can affect the final result. The pronounced grain of a watercolour paper, for example, breaks up the line and thus reduces the strength of the drawing. Charcoal is a medium that should be used decisively; it lends itself to strong, emphatic statements. For that reason it is best to work simply – summarizing the basic shapes and structure rather than getting bogged down with detail.

Above: Caravaggio: Octavio Leoni. This charcoal drawing relies on tonal contrast rather than a linear construction. The rich intensity of the dark areas suggests the famous artist's violent life.

Stick charcoal is brittle and comes in varying thicknesses. The charcoal made from branches of the vine are the finest in quality. Compressed charcoal is short and stubby and made from compressed charcoal powder. Charcoal pencils are easy to handle and break less often than stick charcoal, but the tones produced tend to be less sensitive. The strong, graphic quality of charcoal can enhance even a poor drawing, but one should guard against any formula for producing striking drawings which are not based on observation. When one has achieved a satisfactory result in a charcoal drawing, it should be sprayed with fixative immediately. An unfixed drawing can be completely ruined by even the slightest brush of a sleeve.

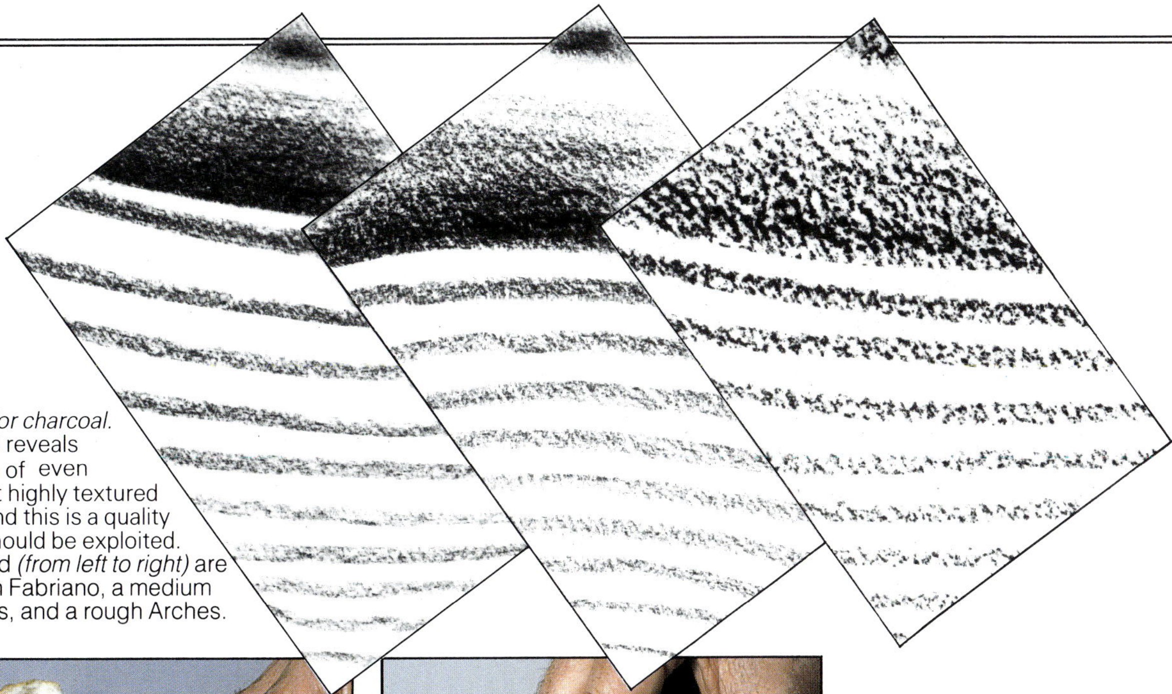

Right:
Papers for charcoal. Charcoal reveals the grain of even the most highly textured paper, and this is a quality which should be exploited. Illustrated *(from left to right)* are a smooth Fabriano, a medium Saunders, and a rough Arches.

Kneaded bread may be used to create soft patches of light.

A soft putty rubber can be used to produce sharp highlights from an area of tone.

PASTELS

BECAUSE colours need to be blended on the paper support, rather than on a separate palette, the colour range of pastels is vast. Well over 500 tints are manufactured by various artists' colourmen. A range of two dozen tints will suffice for most purposes; additional tints can be bought when needed. Graded in soft, medium and hard, the sticks tend to be used up fairly quickly, especially when working intensely with compacted colour. So colours constantly need replacing.

Toned and coloured papers, such as Fabriano or Swedish Ingres, make excellent paper supports. One way of understanding colour values in pastel is to work on

Below: The effect of working on different surfaces. From left to right: flock paper, sandpaper, canvas, and Ingres paper.

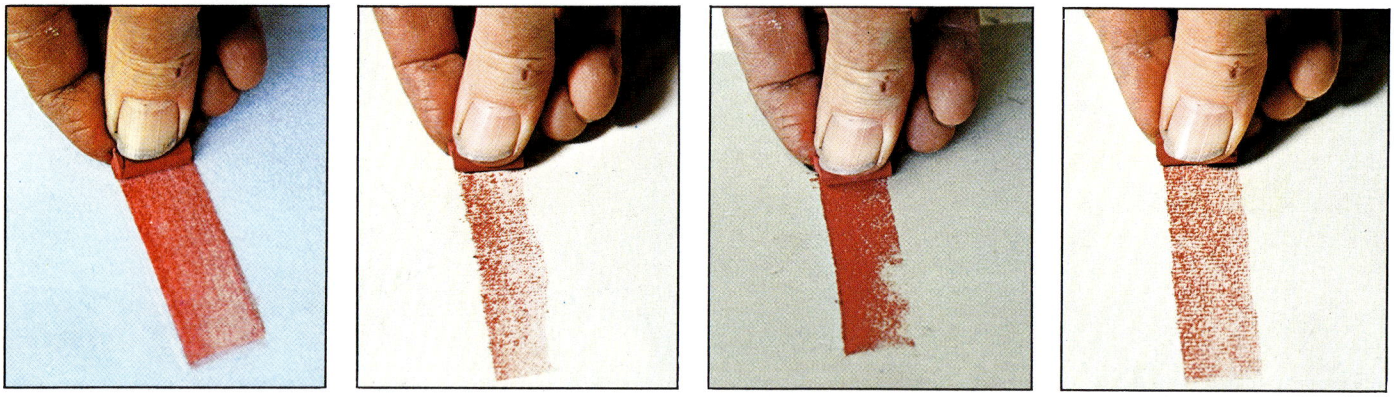

dark-coloured paper – brown or even black. All the light areas in your drawing will then have to be imposed on the dark ground with lighter tints of pastel – working from dark to light, which is a reversal of the normal painting process.

It takes some time to adjust to the idea of blending colour on the surface of the paper and in your first drawings it is advisable to limit the number of colours to four or five from the same colour range – yellow, ochre, terracotta, burnt umber and dark brown or, if you prefer, a range of cool colours. Your first drawings will then be essentially monochromatic and it will be easier to understand tonal values.

The harder the pigment is pressed into the surface of the paper, the more dense the tone will become. But a great deal of surface manipulation of tones can be achieved by spreading and pushing the pigment over a wider area with a finger or a torchon. A gentle touch is sometimes needed to fuse delicate tones together. Preliminary drawing can be carried out in charcoal.

Fixing is done after various stages, or when the drawing is completed.

Oil pastel is really a species of oil painting and it offers much greater resistance than chalk pastel. Turpentine can be used as a thinning agent or to create washes over the drawing. The colour can be scraped away with the edge of a blade and reworked.

Above: Various effects of oil pastels.

Left: Drawing with a paper stoop or 'torchon'. The tip of the torchon is used to blend chalk pastels into soft delicate tones, particularly in flesh tints. It can also be dipped into powdered pastel.

Cadmium yellow

Lemon yellow

Permanent yellow

Yellow ochre

Cobalt violet

The colours illustrated here are those most generally available, and also the most permanent. From this range one can select a personal palette; a range of colours more suited to one's own particular requirements. It is better to start with a few colours in order to gain experience of mixing colours. White is added to make body colour.

Cobalt blue

Cerulean blue

Ultramarine

Monastral (phthalocyanine) blue

Cobalt

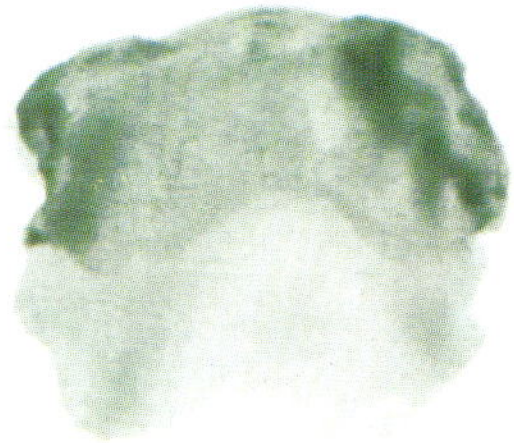

Terre verte

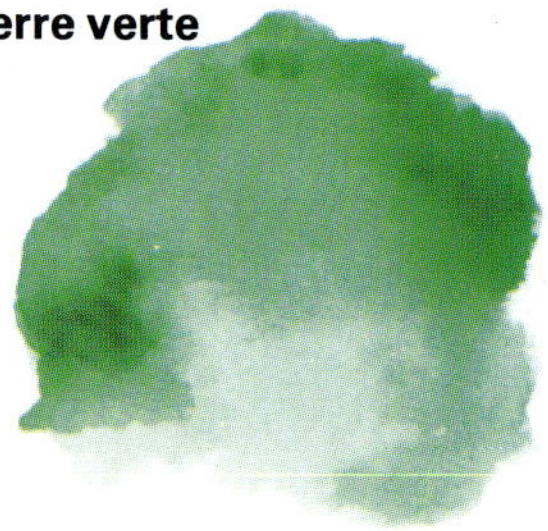

Viridian

WATERCOLOUR

THE important characteristic of watercolour is that the transparent glazes of colour appear to be luminous when applied to a white ground. (This luminosity is lost when darker grounds are used.) Tonal values are determined by the amount of water used to dilute the raw pigment. The French, who refer to watercolour as the 'English method', often prefer to add white paint, which makes the glazes of colour opaque. The only difference between watercolour and gouache is the addition in gouache of white to the transparent colour. It sometimes happens that one needs a combination of pure watercolour

Cadmium red

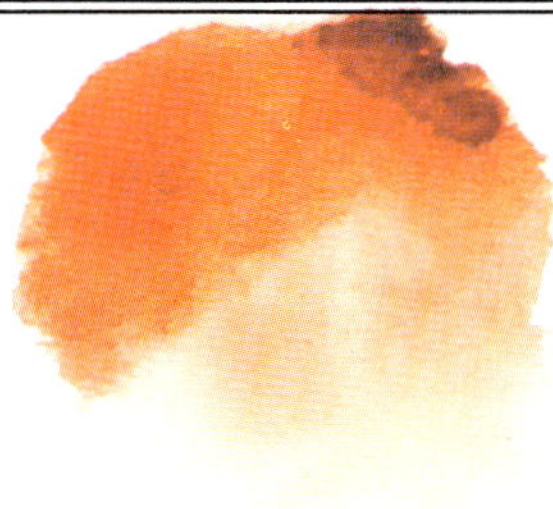

Burnt sienna

Ivory black

Alizarin crimson

Raw sienna

Lamp black

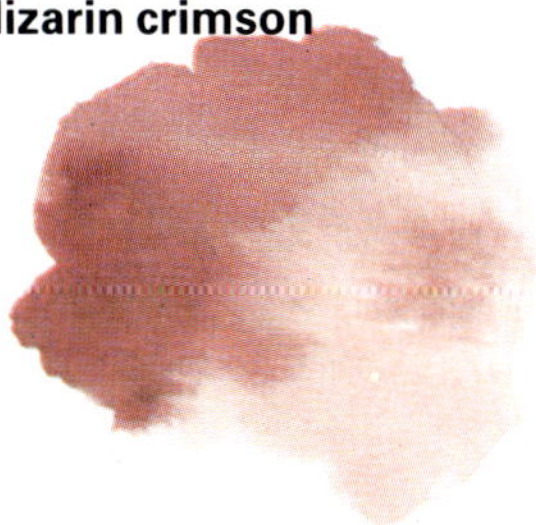

Indian red

Burnt umber

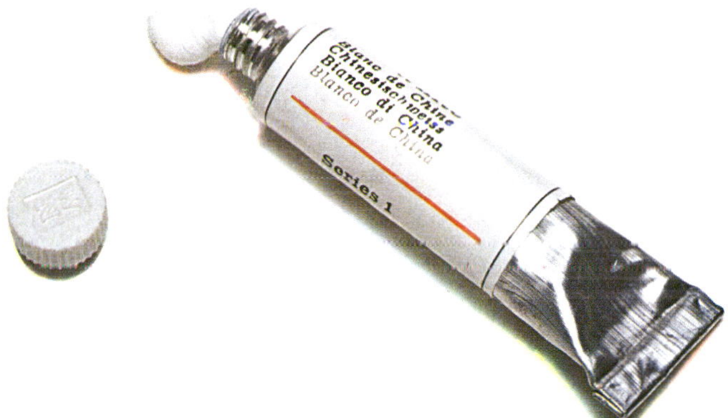

Light red

Raw umber

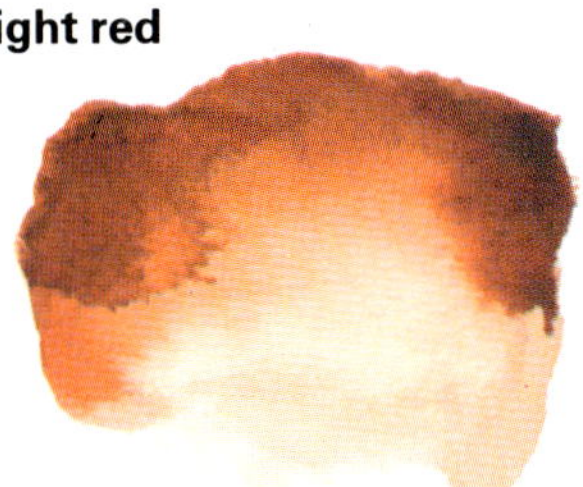

Venetian red

and gouache. In dealing with architecture and water, for instance, or in chalkland landscapes, where all the colours tend to be muted neutrals which are influenced by the presence of chalk.

The powdered pigments are bound in gum arabic, which is soluble in water. Watercolour pigment prepared commercially rarely contains enough gum, and it is useful wherever possible to have your water container filled with a mixture of distilled water and gum arabic. Pigments can be divided into two main groups, mineral and organic, and may be further subdivided as follows:

Mineral

The earth colours: yellow ochre, terre verte, natural ultra-

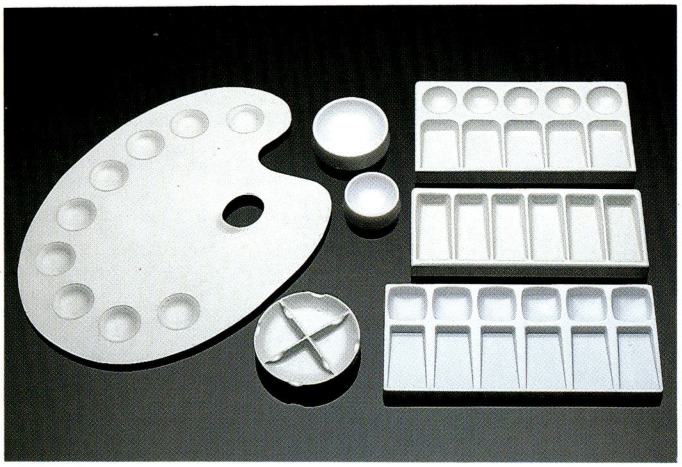

marine
Artificial: Cobalt blue, viridian, cadmium
Organic
Animal: Indian yellow, sepia, carmine
Vegetable: The madders, indigo, sap green
Artificial: Prussian blue

The range of colours in your watercolour box should relate to your personal needs. It is therefore, better to purchase the box and cakes of colour separately. A 12-colour palette will meet the needs of most painters. Pigments which are bound in gum tend to be less permanent than those mixed with oil, and most manufacturers code the various colours according to their degree of permanence.

The following palette was used by Paul Nash and is a useful guide for selecting your own palette.

Red	**Blue**	**Yellow**
Vermillion	Cobalt	Yellow ochre
Light red	Cerulean	Naples yellow
India red	Ultramarine	Lemon yellow
Rosemadder		Chrome yellow
Green	**Brown**	Ivory black
Cobalt	Burnt sienna	Chinese white
Viridian	Raw sienna	Paines grey
Terre verte	Raw umber	Sepia

Above left: Palettes for use in the studio. Usually they are heavy ceramic or plastic, and can be bought in a variety of sizes.

Above: Watercolour can be bought in liquid form though the colours tend to be more fugitive. Round cakes of colour are popular though the colour range is limited.

WASHES AND COLOUR MIXING

Too much emphasis is placed on the handling of watercolour. Although exercises in applying gradated washes are useful to some extent, the best way to learn to handle watercolour is to work directly from nature. All too often one sees blue skies, for instance, made up of superbly gradated washes which bear little relationship to the rest of the painting. Essentially, there are two main approaches to watercolour. One can begin with a preliminary drawing in pencil or from the start with a loaded brush. Each method has its pitfalls. If the linear statement is too dominant, there is a tendency merely to fill in colour in the areas determined by the drawn lines. On the other hand, colour masses which simply merge into each other are difficult to control. It is essential to establish a homogeneous relationship between the drawn lines and the washes of colour. Pencil lines can usually be partially cancelled out by washes of colour, as can a preliminary drawing with brush

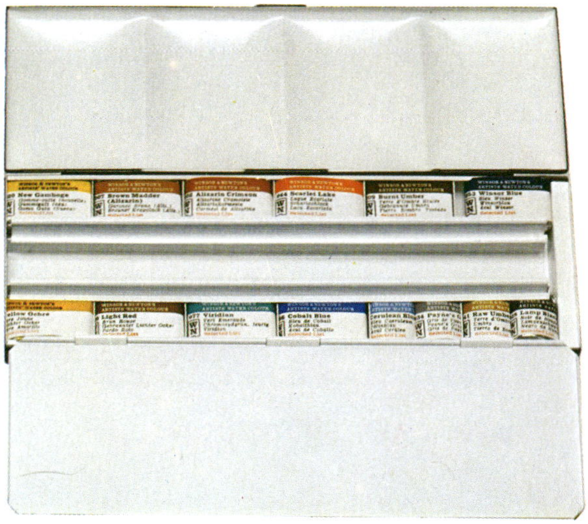

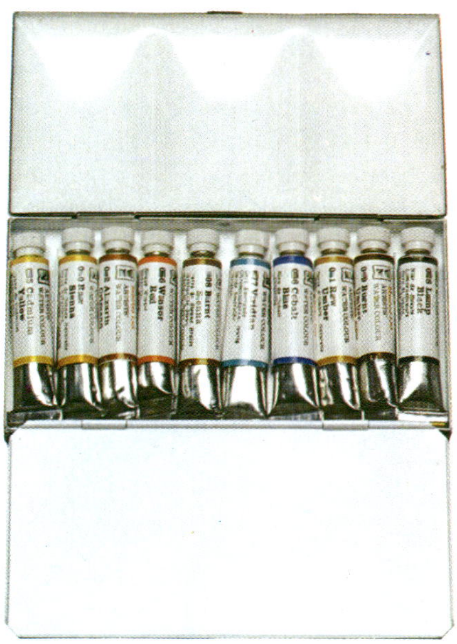

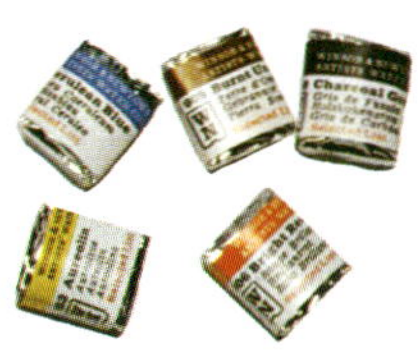

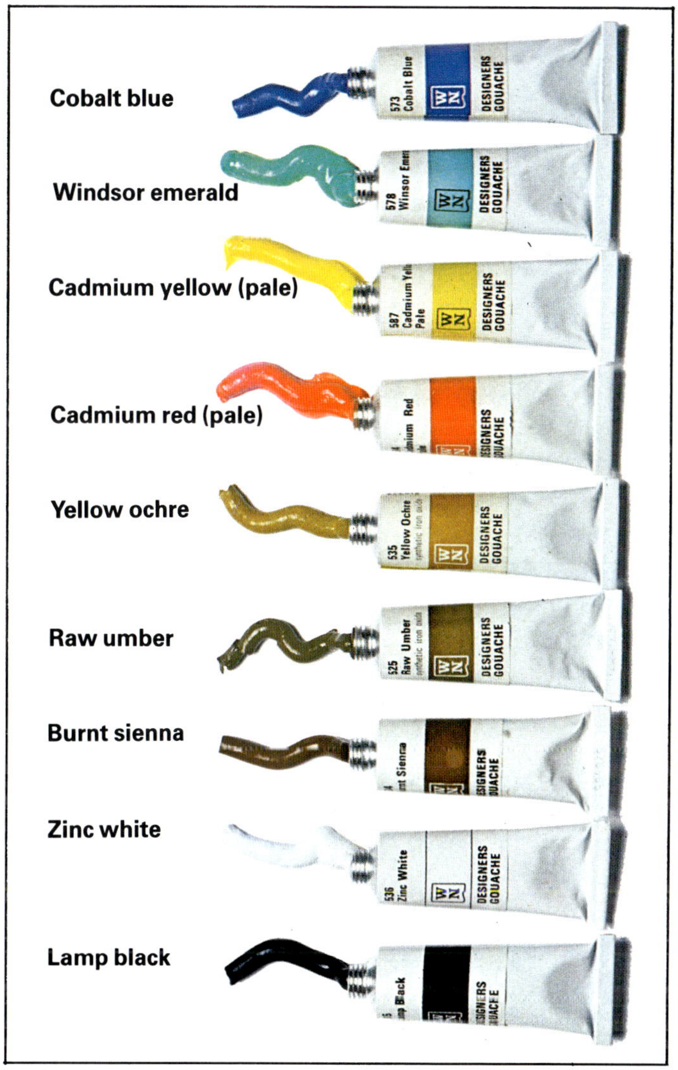

Left and above: Ideally, the semi-moist cakes of colour produced by manufacturers such as Winsor & Newton are of the best quality. Tubes of watercolour can be used on their own or to supplement the colours in a paintbox. Pocket watercolours are ideal for sketching and avoid the burden of carrying too much equipment. Gouache or body colour comes in tubes and the colour range is extensive.

and watercolour. Alternatively, pen and watercolour work quite well together. Again the subject might determine the best way of working – architectural subjects might work best with a combination of pencil or pen and colour washes, whereas plant studies or pure landscape might be best dealt with using a brush for both the drawing and the planes of colour. Make sure that you have enough water to replenish the waterpot from time to time – nothing is worse than trying to get a clean colour with muddy water. Try also to carry an extra plate or saucer for colour mixing, so that sufficient quantities of colour can be mixed for large areas of flat colour in the painting.

GOUACHE

Gouache paints are opaque and tend to dry lighter than when first applied. The pigment is ground together with a white filler which gives them their opacity. They have been in use for a much longer period than watercolour,

Above: The main characteristic which distinguishes watercolour from other media is that the colour value is reduced by adding water only.

Above: Albrecht Dürer: Young Hare. An extremely fine, detailed study. Dürer probably began by laying dark and light washes to establish the fundamental form. Over this, he used fine water colour lines to a well-planned design. He would have used white gouache for the highlights.

although recently they have been replaced to some extent by acrylic paints, which are also water soluble. Nevertheless, gouache is a very adaptable medium with a wide range of colours available. The colour can be used thickly or it may be watered down to a fine wash. It can be used on both white paper and coloured paper, on cardboard and even on manila wrapping paper.

The opacity of gouache, and the fact that light colours can be laid on dark, makes it very different in character from watercolour. It can be used in varying consistencies, but there is no point in using it thinly as a substitute for watercolour. It should be exploited for its own inherent qualities. The colours can be very rich, especially when they are close in tone. It is common practice to work from neutral colours towards the darkest tones. Dry brushwork – where the brush is starved of colour – is another technique which works well in gouache. The surface of the paint can be scraped down with the edge of a sharp blade and gum arabic can be added to give the paint surface a slight glaze.

Right: *Oils*
Oils used as media for oil paint *(from left)*: pure (cold-pressed) linseed oil; raw linseed oil; refined linseed oil; stand oil (also linseed); poppy oil; walnut oil.

Left: Appledore: Thomas Girtin This small Devon fishing village is almost unchanged since Girtin painted it. He produced this painting using only five colours carefully overlaid to create subtle tones.

OIL PAINTING

FOR almost 500 years oil painting has been the medium most widely used by artists. There are a variety of reasons for this, but primarily it is because the use of oil paints can affect the artist's intentions in a way that is not possible in any other medium. The mixing and manipulation of oil paint can, in themselves, suggest uses to an artist. If, for example, one compares the highly charged brushstrokes of a Van Gogh painting with the wonderfully fine, luminous glazes of a Turner seascape, it becomes clear that oil paint can be used to give expression to very different levels of feeling.

Oil paint is made by mixing powdered pigments with certain types of drying vegetable oils – linseed or poppy oil. The hardening of the paint is gradual and depends on the nature of the drying oil, the proportion of it used in relation to pigment, and the room temperature and humidity. This slow drying process is a distinct advantage to the artist especially when producing a work which requires a number of sittings, such as a portrait or still-life. Another important factor is that even when dry the colours retain their tonality and do not become lighter. By painting wet on wet over a period of time, a very subtle range of colour can be achieved. Anyone who has seen an original Rembrandt portrait will wonder how it is possible to achieve such luminosity and depth with such limited means. By varying the proportions of oil and thinners (linseed oil and turpentine) one can obtain a wide variety of paint qualities – from thin, almost transparent glazes, to a thick impasto which is more akin to a sculptural low-relief.

The use of oil to bind pigment was probably developed in the Low Countries in the fifteenth century. In Venice, however, it is said that oil paint was used to combat the effect on wall paintings of the high humidity and general dampness from the canals and the Adriatic. Giovanni Bellini, Titian and Giorgione worked in oil in Venice and

1
Artists' Oil Colour
Permanent Magenta (Quinacridone)
209 SL
Magenta Permanent
Permanentmagenta
Magenta Permanente
2
Artists' Oil Colour
Prussian Blue
127 SL
Bleu de Prusse
Preussischblau
Azul de Prusia
Blu di Prussia
3
Artists' Oil Colour
Winsor Blue
168 SL
Bleu Winsor
Winsorblau
Azul Winsor
Blu Winsor
4
Artists' Oil Colour
French Ultramarine
149 SL
Outremer Français
Französisches Ultramarin
Ultramar Francés
Oltremare Francese
5
Artists' Oil Colour
Cobalt Blue
203 SL
Bleu de Cobalt
Kobaltblau
Azul de Cobalto
Blu di Cobalto
6
Artists' Oil Colour
Cerulean Blue
202 SL
Bleu Caeruleum
Cölinblau
Azul Cerúleo
Blu Celeste
7
Artists' Oil Colour
Oxide of Chromium
226 SL
Oxyde de Chrome
Chromoxydgrün
Oxido de Cromo
Ossido di Cromio
15
Artists' Oil Colour
Raw Sienna
128 SL
Terre de Sienne Naturelle
Siena Natürliche
Tierra de Siena Natural
Terra di Siena Naturale
16
MADE IN ENGLAND
Series 6
17
Artists' Oil Colour
Cadmium Red
219 SL
Rouge de Cadmium
Kadmiumrot
Rojo Cadmio
Rosso di Cadmio
18
Series 2
19
Artists' Oil Colour
Rose Madder Genuine
232 SL
Garance Rose
Rosa Krapplack
Rosa de Garanza
Garanza Rosa
20
Artists' Oil Colour
Venetian Red
135 SL
Rouge de Venise
Venetianischrot
Rojo de Venecia
Rossi di Venezia
21

Oil Colours
This selection represents the most widely-used oil colours: **1** Permanent magenta, a violet red **2** Prussian blue **3** Monastral blue **4** French ultramarine **5** Cobalt blue **6** Cerulean blue **7** Chrome oxide **8** Terre verte **9** Monastral green **10** Chrome yellow **11** Cadmium yellow **12** Aureolin **13** Gold ochre **14** Yellow ochre **15** Raw sienna **16** Vermilion **17** Cadmium red **18** Alizarin crimson **19** Rose madder **20** Venetian red **21** Burnt sienna **22** Vandyke brown **23** Raw umber **24** Burnt umber **25** Titanium white **26** Lamp black.

Above: Snowstorm: William Turner (1775–1851)
This painting demonstrates the wonderful atmospheric effects that Turner obtained by the use of transparent glazes of oil colour.

demonstrated a wonderful command of the medium. But it is in the work of Rembrandt that the exquisite drama of contrasting light and dark modelling reaches the height of genius.

Whereas oil painting was considered to be essentially a studio-based activity, Constable and other painters in the eighteenth century used specially prepared oil colours, sold by artists' colourmen in skin bladders, to make colour sketches directly from nature. The tubes of oil paint that we use today were pioneered in the nineteenth century and made it possible for the Impressionists to work from direct observation in the countryside with a new sense of freedom, each according to his own method.

The artist's palette – the selection of colours he chooses to employ – is largely a matter of personal choice. To begin with it is better to concentrate on a limited range of colours – this will encourage you to experiment with mixing colours

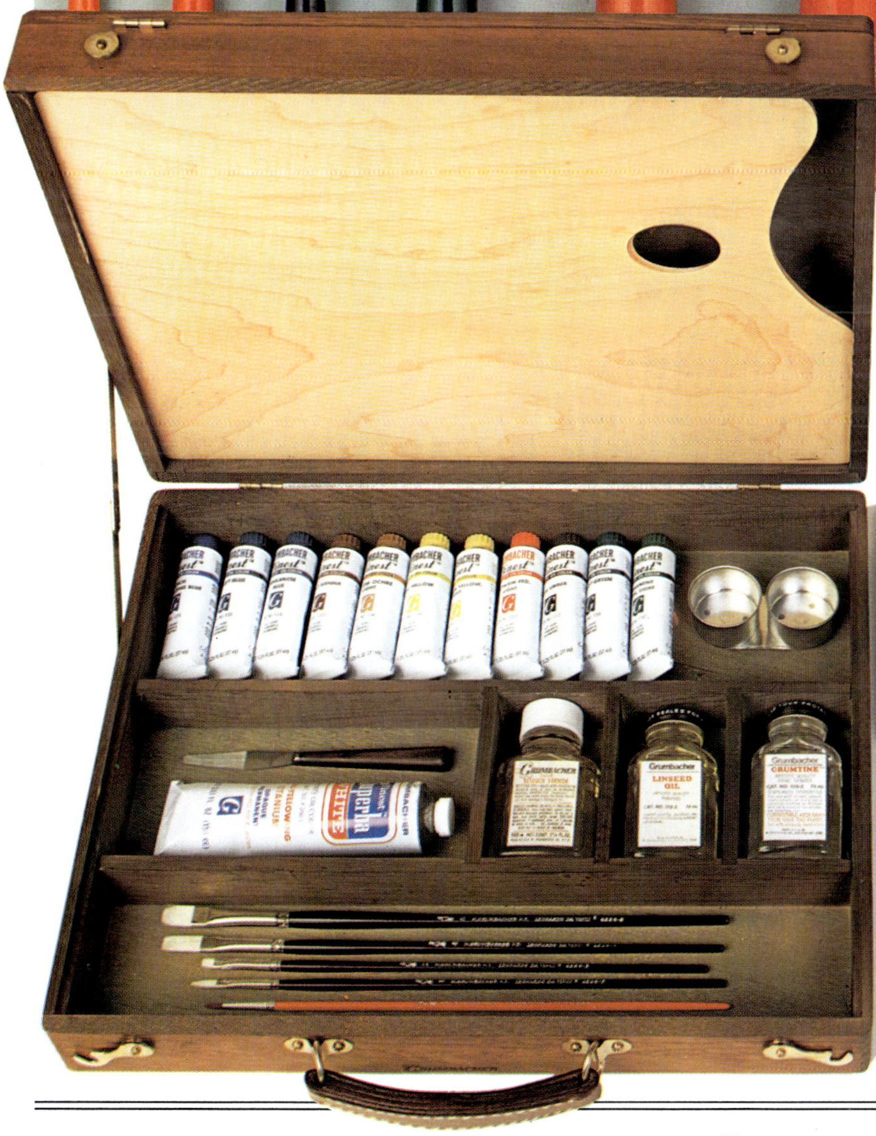

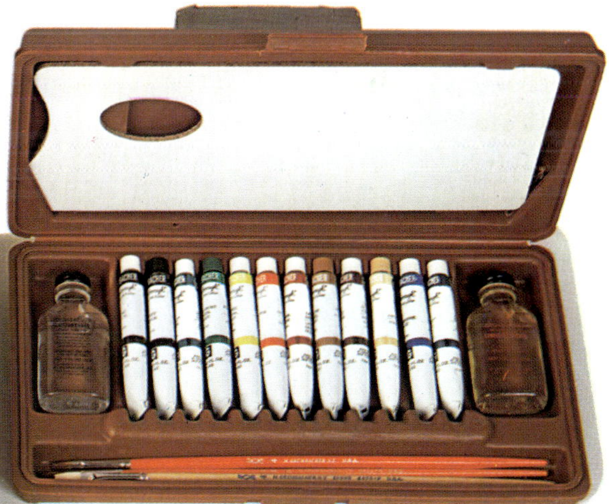

Above: Types of oil painting brush. The best brushes are sable or hogshair but recently the traditional materials are being replaced by synthetic hair.

Above and left: Oil paint sets are useful in the studio, but can be too cumbersome for landscape painting; most painters now prefer to carry their equipment in lighter shoulder bags.

and to make discoveries about colour in the process of mixing. A basic palette to start with might include the following colours:

- Flake white
- Titanium white
- Lamp black
- Yellow ochre
- Naples yellow
- Burnt umber
- Venetian red
- Cadmium red
- Cadmium orange
- Cerulean blue
- Ultramarine
- Viridian
- Cobalt blue

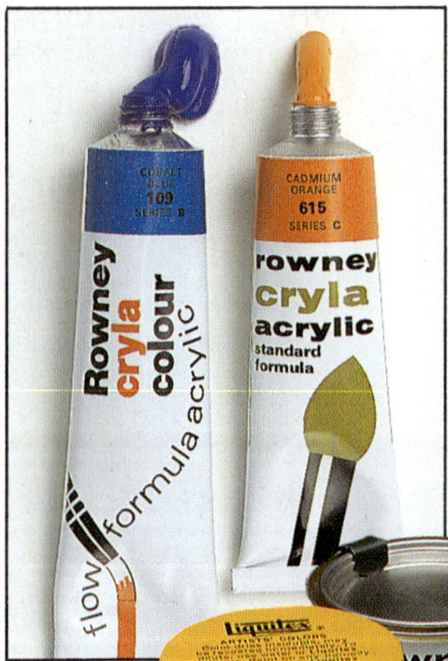

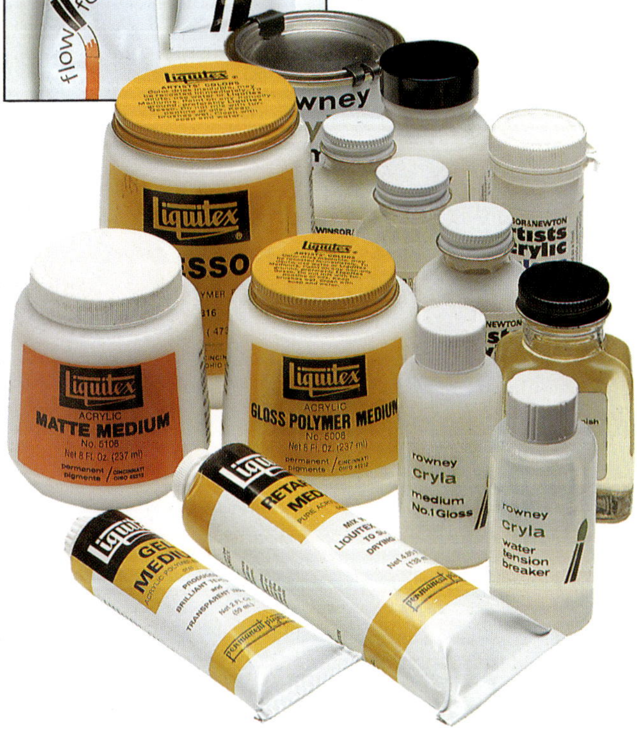

Left: Rowney Cryla colours are just one example of the many different types of acrylic paint available.
Below: Mediums are used with acrylic paints to give a heavier impasto, to add gloss, or conversely to make more matt, and to make them more liquid. Gesso primers can be used for both acrylic and egg-tempera paints.
Opposite: Coloured pigments. The rich colour in its raw state is the basis for making tempera paints.

ACRYLICS

ACRYLIC paints have been in general use for only about 20 years or so. They are made by combining coloured pigment with a synthetic resin. Acrylics are water soluble and dry very rapidly. One particular advantage for the beginner is that because no traditions nor established techniques prevail, one is free to make use of the medium in a completely personal way. Acrylics can be used in thin washes of colour or as a thicker impasto. For those artists who previously tended to combine watercolour with gouache, acrylics offer an alternative method. They can be painted on almost any surface – from canvas to cardboard – and even on unprimed surfaces. They are ideal for use on a large scale, and are especially suitable for mural painting, since they do not crack or gather dust so readily as other paints. A completed painting can safely be cleaned from time to time with soapy water. Acrylics are being used increasingly by both students and professional painters.

TEMPERA

TEMPERA, or egg-tempera as it is generally known, is paint made by blending pure colour pigment with egg yolk. It is thinned with distilled water, which evaporates once the colour has hardened. Tempera is one of the most permanent media available. It is essentially an emulsion made up of oil and water constituents. When the paint is dry it cannot be dissolved, even with hot water.

Tempera is characterized chiefly by the dryness of the colour. It does not yellow or darken with age. The preparation involved in mixing it can be formidable, but the results more than justify a little patience. It is possible to purchase egg-tempera ready-mixed in tubes, but most tempera artists prefer to mix their own colours. The coloured pigment is first ground with water into a soft paste (the coloured paste can be stored in airtight containers). Mix the tempera immediately before use in an equal quantity of pigment to egg yolk. The white of the egg should be removed altogether. The egg is first cracked over a bowl, preferably with a knife so that it breaks evenly. Allow the white of the egg to run into the bowl, holding the yolk back. Then pass the yolk from one half of the shell to the other several times – this gets rid of the remaining white. The yolk can then be punctured and poured into a cup. Add three spoonfuls of cold water and stir. The mixture is then poured into a stoppered container and thoroughly shaken to emulsify yolk and water. Then mix equal parts with the coloured pigment paste to make the tempera. As with gouache the paint is thinned for use with water.

Left: Detail of a mural in the Graduate School of Business Studies, London: Leonard Rosoman
This painting shows how acrylic paints can be used to cover large areas without any undue loss of paint quality. All the textural richness, the delicate washes of colour are retained. When the mural becomes dusty it can be washed with warm water without damaging the surface. The artist made a detailed study in acrylic gouache prior to starting the mural painting. The main details were painted in raw umber using a half-inch hog's hair brush. The larger areas of colour were applied with 3"/7.5cm brushes. The completed mural is 10ft × 30ft/3 metres × 9 metres.

Below: Pigments for tempera painting: **1** Zinc white **2** Titanium white **3** French Ultramarine **4** Cerulean blue **5** Viridian **6** Cadmium yellow **7** Scarlet lake **8** Cadmium red **9** Venetian red **10** Indian red **11** and **13** Burnt and raw sienna **12** Burnt umber **14** Yellow ochre **15** Raw umber **16** Ivory black

1

2

3

1 Dry powdered pigment is transferred to a small jar.
2 Distilled water is added sparingly to make a thick paste.
3 Replace the top securely and shake the bottle vigorously.

1

2

3

1 The egg is broken and the yolk separated by allowing the white to drain through the fingers in a bowl.
2 Make the yolk dry by passing from one hand to the other. Hold the yolk carefully and make an incision to allow the liquid to run into a glass container.
3 Distilled water is added and stirred to a consistency of cream.

1

2
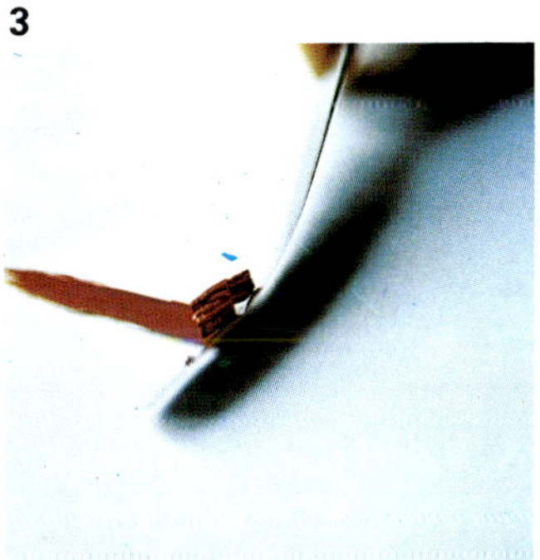
3

1 The pigment and egg yolk binder are now blended together with a palette knife.
2 The paint is tested on a piece of glass.
3 When dry the paint is scraped off and stored for use. If it is too dry, add more egg.

There are other recipes for tempera, using either linseed oil and glue or gum arabic and wax. Many early manuscripts were decorated with illustrations drawn with egg tempera and it is worth noting that not only have they survived well, but in many cases they look as fresh as the day they were painted. Giotto and Botticelli used tempera for fresco painting. That is why there are so many fine examples of their work still intact. Today artists tend to use a gesso ground. Hardboard can be a most suitable support – some artists prefer to paste cotton or linen on to hardboard before priming with gesso. Gesso primer can be bought ready-mixed or made from gilder's white mixed with size. At least four coats of primer are required, allowing approximately half an hour drying-time between each coat. The surface can then be smoothed with a damp sponge, and when dry rubbed with a fine sandpaper.

8 9 10 11 12 13 14 15 16

Below: Equipment needed for Tempera.
The palette should be preferably glass or paper so that the residue of egg can be easily removed. The eye-droppers are used for transferring the pigment paste and egg to the palette. The bowls are useful when mixing larger quantities of paint.

Right: Wide brushes are sometimes used for laying large areas of dilute tempera. They should be fairly soft. Those illustrated are: ox hair, bristle, white bristle, camel hair, and badger hair.

Right: Tempera paint can be mixed prior to use, or bought ready mixed in tubes.

Primer for Tempera.
The size is mixed with 1 part rabbit skin glue to 10 parts water. To make the gesso ground for tempera, gilders white and zinc white are added. Linseed oil is also used to prevent cracking.

1 Making size. The size crystals (10 parts water to one part size) are soaked overnight.

2 The size is heated in a double boiler until all the crystals are dissolved. Do not boil.

Gesso
1 1 part whiting is mixed with 1 part of Titanium white.

2 With the powders well mixed together, prepare an equal quantity of size (equal in volume).

3 Gradually add the size to the powder to make a thick paste. Avoid air bubbles.

4 Continue adding size until the gesso becomes creamy. It can be further strained through muslin to remove any lumps.

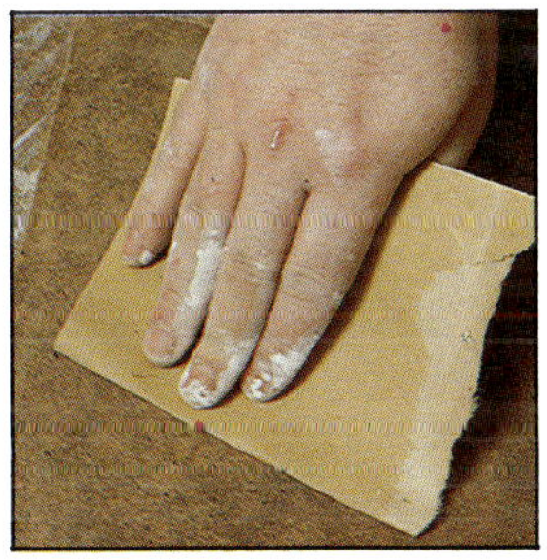

Preparing a panel
1 Roughen the surface of the board with sandpaper.

2 Apply a coat of size to both sides of the panel – allow the size to dry thoroughly.

3 Apply a thin coat of gesso. When dry apply a second coat.

4 Continue to apply up to six coats of gesso. When dry, rub the surface with fine sandpaper.

5 Finally polish the surface gently with a damp rag to make it perfectly smooth for painting.

CHAPTER 2

DRAWING

DRAWING

MANY thousands of years ago paleolithic man made drawings on the walls of caves such as those in Altamira, Spain. They are drawings of acute sensitivity and show how early man described the animal life which he hunted. Drawing, then, is the most spontaneous way of communicating our view of the world around us.

There are, of course, many different kinds of drawing – architects and engineers use drawings for purely practical purposes. The artist, however, gives his work a significance beyond description. He uses drawing as a means of realizing his sensations, expressing his feelings about a particular object, person or place. The quality of the drawn line bears the imprint of his perception and sensitivity towards his subject. If we compare, for example, a perspective drawing by Canaletto with a figure study by Rembrandt, we are at once impressed by the degree of fidelity in Canaletto's rendering of architectural detail. But the Rembrandt drawing is endowed with a different delicacy of feeling, the implications of which are felt rather than described. The quest for rendering fine detail in a drawing reveals a certain kind of temperament; so does a more vigorous form of drawing. The importance of drawing, therefore, lies in the personal vision it expresses.

We draw with a reserve of knowledge and that knowledge can be gained only by intensive observation. The more we get into the habit of drawing frequently from direct observations, the more we sharpen our visual awareness generally. When we talk of accuracy in a drawing, we are really talking about things which are both accurately observed and accurately drawn. We attempt to relate detail to detail and to create a sense of three-dimensional qualities – volume, solidity and recession – on the flat surface of the paper. To draw accurately really means to be true to one's vision. Factual representation is not the only criterion in drawing: every artist has his own individual way of explaining what he can see. If he is moved emotionally by a subject this should be revealed in the quality of the drawing. Can anyone who looks at a drawing of a young child by Renoir doubt his extreme sensitivity towards the subject?

Above right: North East Corner of Piazza Zan Marco, Venice: Antonio Canaletto Perspective was a vital element in all of Canaletto's drawings and paintings. He pioneered different systems of perspective drawing, and made use of a camera obscura for tracing fine architectural detail.

Right: Portrait of a lady: Jean-Auguste Ingres This drawing is characteristic of the artist's subtle use of line and tone. The refinement of detail in the rendering of the head, contrasts with the more lucid treatment of the dress.

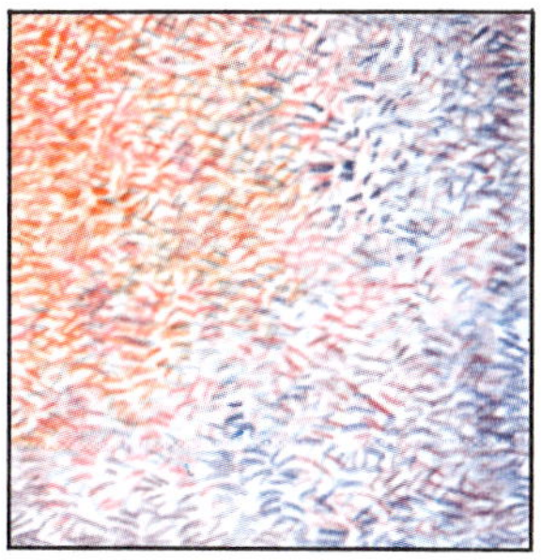

A web of colour made by using different coloured pencils in short overlapping strokes.

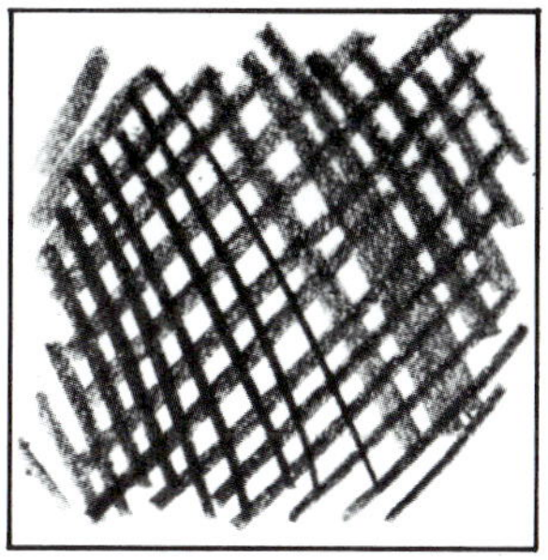

The grit-like texture made with a wax pencil such as a Chinagraph.

Soft atmospheric tones created by blending crayon dust.

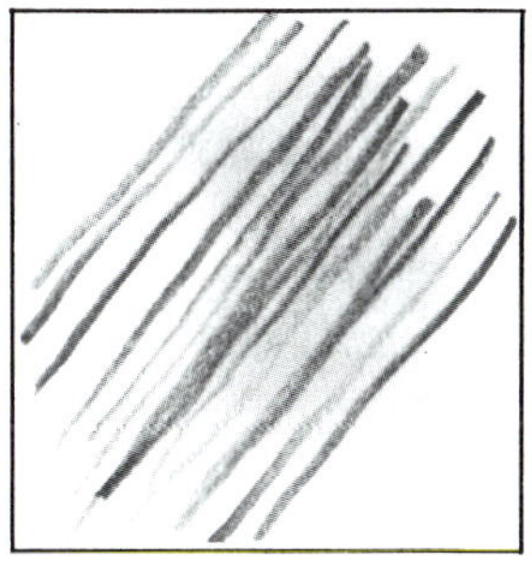

The lines of a 4H pencil are softened by burnishing with a finger.

A soft 4B pencil drawn over coloured crayon.

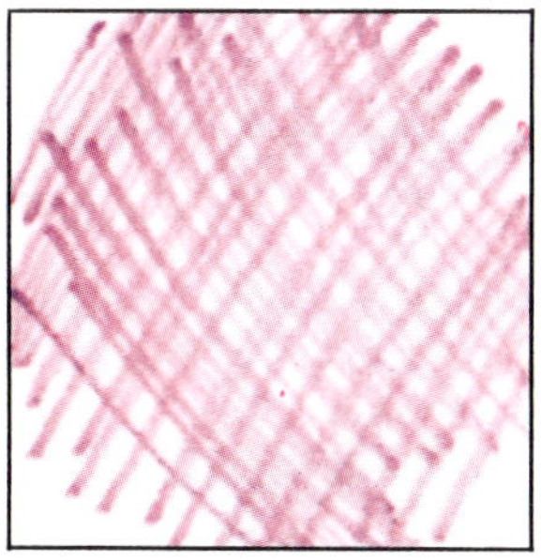

The line of a Caran d'Ache pencil blurred by first damping the watercolour paper.

Black marks transferred from carbon paper.

Blended tones of Caran d'Ache pencils.

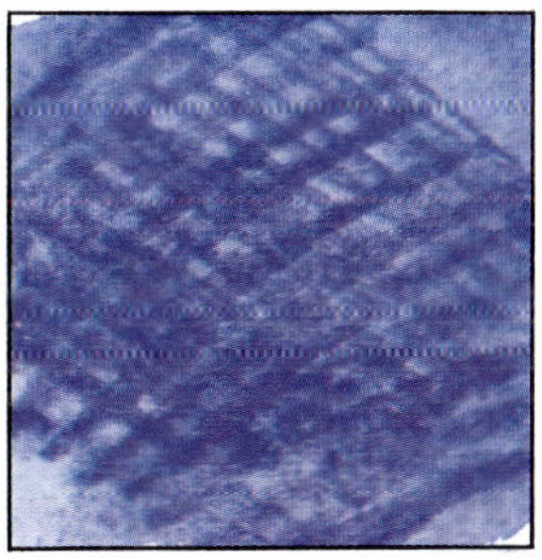

A wash dilutes the cross-hatched lines of a Caran d'Ache pencil.

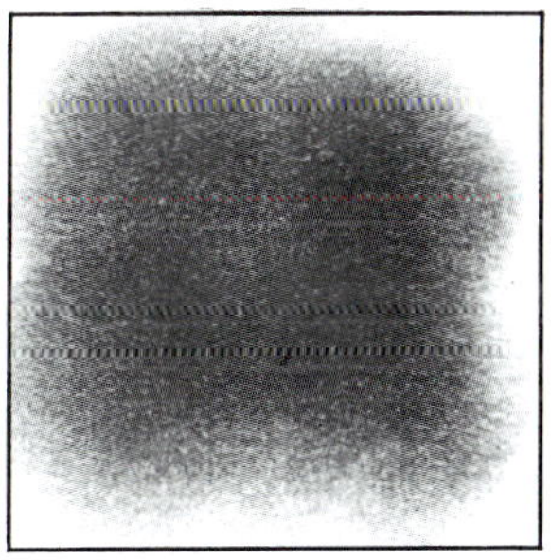

Soft tones produced by rubbing graphite dust into the paper.

Gradations of colour made with coloured crayons reveal the texture of the paper.

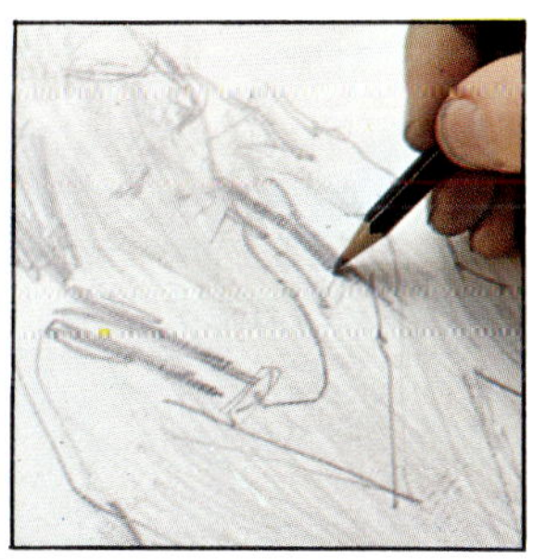

2B and 5B pencils used in the same drawing.

Using a 2B pencil to block in tone.

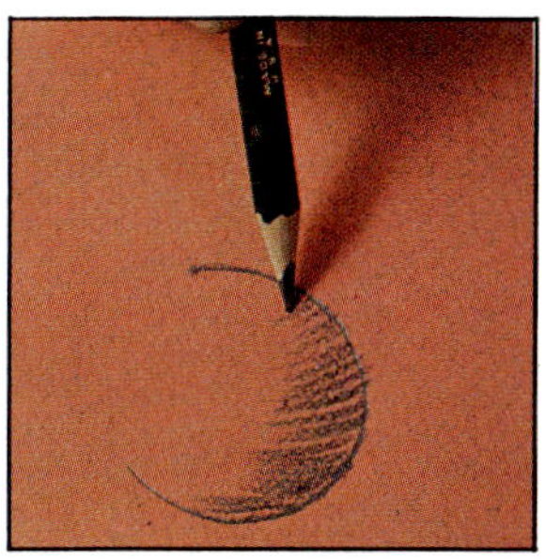

Coloured paper makes a good ground for tonal drawing.

Highlights are added using a white pencil.

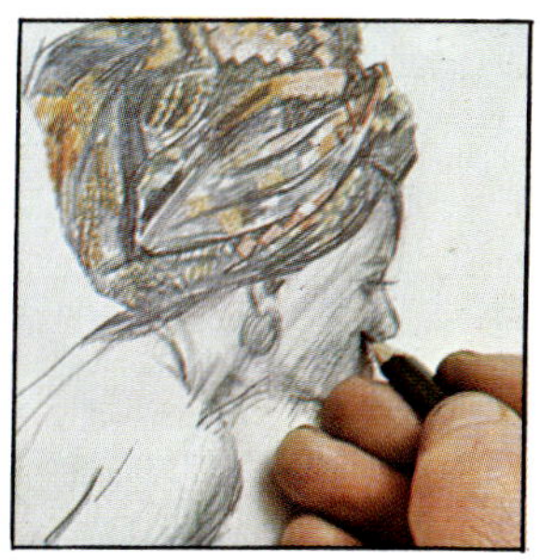

Combining black and coloured pencils.

Above: Dancer adjusting her slipper: Edgar Degas
A beautifully composed drawing in pencil and charcoal on a pink-toned paper.

Above: Still-life: Christopher Chamberlain
An exquisitely-composed drawing which makes good use of charcoal as a medium for creating subtle changes in tonal contrast.

Above: Portrait: Leonardo da Vinci
The fine detail in this drawing is produced with a silverpoint on cream paper.

Above: Jane Seymour: Hans Holbein the Younger
Coloured chalks were drawn over the fine lines made with a metal point.

Right: Seated figure
A direct charcoal study drawn as a single statement.

Above: A soft 4B pencil was used to block in the tones in this figure study.

Right: Beach Umbrella: David Hockney
The dark shaded background helps to define the simple vertical shape of the folded umbrella.

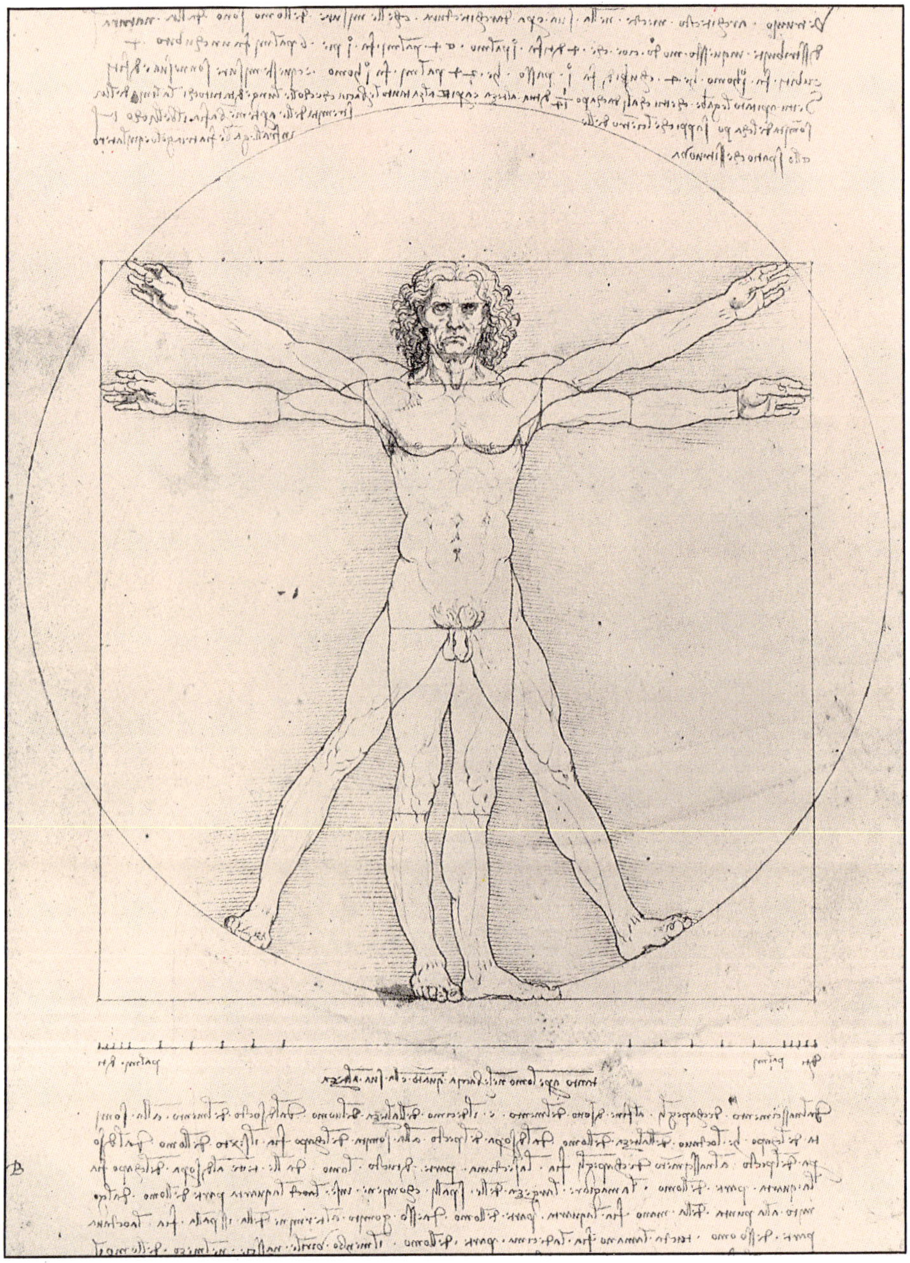

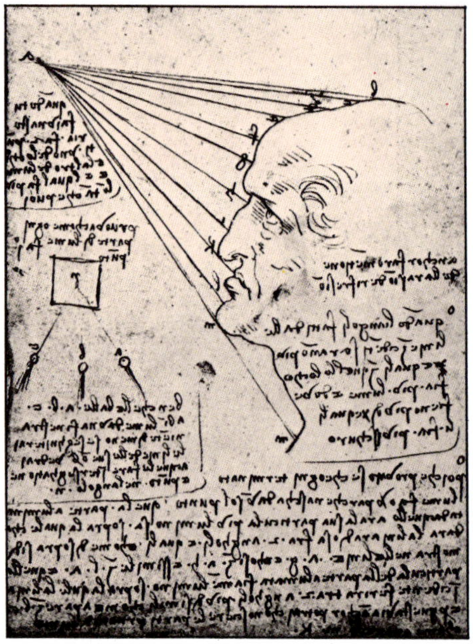

Left and above: The proportions of man: Leonardo da Vinci
The natural proportions of the human body were sometimes used in relation to the division of space in drawing and painting.

Below: Proportions of the hand: Albrecht Dürer
Early painters made a thorough study of the laws of proportion.

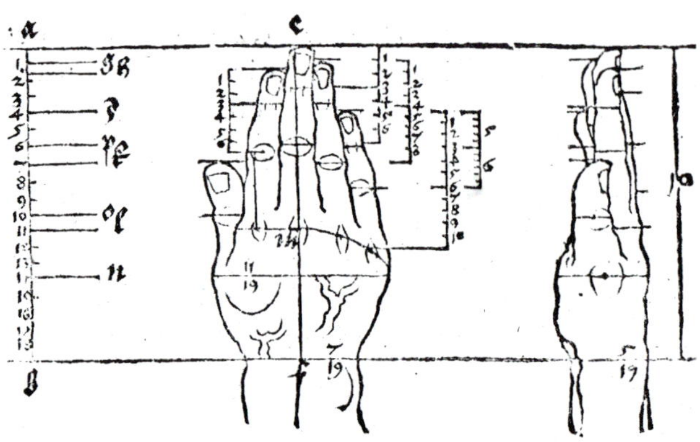

Above: Seated female nude from the back: Rembrandt van Rijn
Working with a reed pen and wash Rembrandt demonstrates his mastery of rendering a succinct statement which is completely convincing.

GIRL READING

THE composition for this drawing is essentially very basic – a seated figure positioned by a window, with a table, a bowl of fruit and flowers. It is a drawing which demonstrates how a single light source influences the tonality and mood of the picture. The particular placement of the figure is important; the light filtering through the window catches the edge of the form, and the other elements of the composition nearest to the window. Without this sense of modelling, without the gradations from light to dark, the composition would appear flat and reduced to two-dimensional pattern. We use shading with short strokes of pastel to create a sense of solidity and to convey the feeling of three-dimensional form on a two-dimensional surface. The atmospheric mood is induced by softly blending colours together either with a finger or with a paper torchon.

Sharpening Pastels **1** Pastels can be given a sharp edge when rubbed gently onto a sheet of sandpaper.

2 Oil pastels are much firmer than chalk pastels and can be sharpened with a knife.

1 The main structure of the drawing is carried out in a single mid-tone colour.

2 Yellow, blue and red are added to establish the main divisions of tone and colour.

3 The tonal contrast between the outside view and the darker interior is heightened by the use of Prussian blue.

All the colours are blended together with softer tones in the shadows to evoke a certain mood and atmosphere in the drawing.

Above left:
Woman ironing: Edgar Degas
This is a pastel drawing on toned paper; the highlights are drawn with white chalk.

Left:
Head of a boy: Andrea del Sarto
A beautifully-modelled face which is expressively drawn with fine lines, sometimes softened with a finger or torchon.

Above:
Woman combing her hair: Edgar Degas
Essentially this is a drawing about movement; the rhythmic flow of the hair and the suggested movement of arms and hand are full of conviction. Degas used charcoal on top of the pastel to emphasize the contours of the figure.

Right:
Maude reading: James McNeill Whistler
A drawing which has been made quickly from direct observation. The charcoal on brown paper has been tentatively highlighted with white chalk.

WOODLAND SCENE

In the drawing, the artist is concerned with the interlocking shapes of the trees, paths and undergrowth. Light falls on the path and leads the eye out of the wood. Careful control was required to get the correct tonal balance – the darkness of the wood is suggested, while at the same time there is a particular spatial relationship between the trees and plants. The artist has used a fairly soft pencil to give emphasis to trees in the foreground.

1 A 2B pencil can be used for delineating the main shapes of trees and also for shading in areas of tone.
2 Light hatching is applied to the drawing to suggest depth and recession. The tones are developed throughout the composition, rather than being concentrated in one area.

3 Individual elements are heightened with broader hatching.
4 The hatching unifies the drawing as shadows are linked between the vertical contours of the trees.

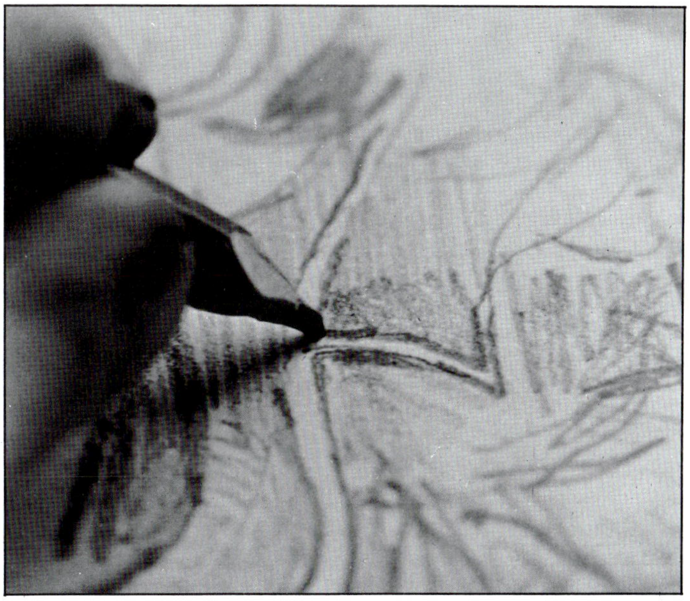

5 Short criss-cross marks suggest movement and rhythm of grass and plants. The tonal balance is critical at this stage of the drawing; if the tone is applied too heavily, it could destroy the unity of the composition as a whole.

6 Some lines are re-stated to bring out particular forms in the landscape.

THREE FIGURE STUDIES

The figures in these drawings appear casual as they engage in inconsequential tasks – a girl teases a cat with a stick, another is busily sewing, while the third peels leaves from a plant. None of the figures appears to be 'posed' for the artist and it is this quality which gives them their charm.

Right: This drawing was made rapidly from direct observation using compressed charcoal on a laid white paper.

Below: The soft tones in the drawing were produced with a wax crayon and a wash of gouache of the same colour.

Opposite: A strong black lithographic pencil was used for the gritty lines in this study.

USING A SKETCHBOOK

Every artist needs to get into the habit of drawing frequently from observation. A sketchbook is rather like a writer's notebook; one is able to put down everyday incidents, colour notes, figure studies and ideas for composition. The sketchbook can be small enough to fit into a coat pocket, or large enough to record a fairly large landscape scene. Quite often, the artist's most interesting work will be found in his sketchbook; the small sketchbooks used by John Constable for instance, reveal a wealth of intimate detail in terms of cloud studies, the effect of light on the landscape, and details of artefacts, such as farm wagons, all of which he used as reference for his larger paintings.

Drawing board with strap
If the artist is sketching a moving subject, a drawing board with a strap attached may well prove useful. The strap is passed around the artist's neck leaving the hands free for work and allowing him or her to walk around.

Right: Firmly bound sketchbooks are used a great deal by artists who build up studio paintings from sketched notes made elsewhere, especially outdoors. Such books are durable and can provide a permanent record of objects and scenes recorded over many years.

1 The artist begins to draw a building, having first decided on a particular viewpoint.

2 He establishes the main vertical and horizontal elements in the drawing first.

3 Local colour is added with coloured pencils.

4 The building appears to be more solid as the drawing develops tonally.

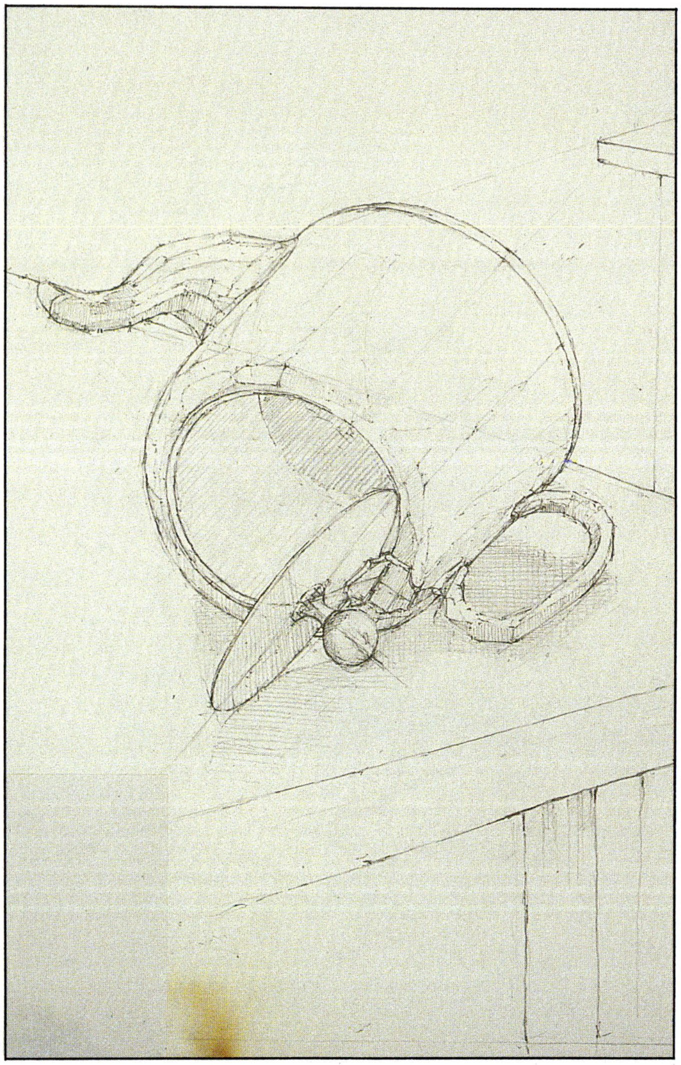

Top: Pen and ink drawing: Tuscany
The sense of intense light is conveyed by the understatement of the drawing. Shadows are indicated without the use of cross-hatching.

Above: The pine and cypress trees for a natural vignette through which the domes and rooftops of Florence are revealed. The broad nib of an old fountain pen produces a rich variety of linear qualities.

Left: Teapot: This drawing in pencil is an example of measured drawing which comes from intense concentration on the proportions of the object.

East Guldeford Church,
Romney Marsh.
A drawing in pen and ink with spatter. The reeds appear as negative shapes painted with white gouache.

Dancer I: Pencil and coloured crayon on toned paper. A drawing made rapidly while the model was resting between sittings.

PASTEL (OIL & CHALK)

CHALK pastels are bound together with gum and white filler. The crumbling particles are pressed into the surface of a suitable support paper. Unlike watercolour or oil paint, the colours are not mixed before being applied to a support. The colour mixing takes place as part of the drawing process itself, by fusing one colour into another. This is done with the finger tip or with a paper-felt stump called a torchon. The colour of chalk pastels are neutralized to some extent by the presence of the white filler. Thus we tend to talk of 'pastel shades'.

Careful examination of a pastel drawing by Degas will reveal his technique of building up colour in a web of opposing chalk strokes. Pastel drawings are distinguished from other drawings by the freshness of their colour. Degas was much influenced by the pastel drawings of Quentin de la Tour, whose work he collected. But he developed his own techniques and often used a semi-transparent paper to produce progressive states of a composition by laying one drawing on top of another, tracing the contours of the first drawing as a basis for the next. By spraying water on to certain parts of an almost completed pastel drawing, he was able to brush certain passages in the drawing into a paste-like texture. Pastel has often been successfully combined with other media; some painters, for instance, first produce an 'under-painting', using oil paint or gouache very thinly, and then gradually build up a pastel drawing on top of it. Degas added pastel to his monotype prints, first painting his subject with oil very thinly on to a copper plate. The image on the plate was transferred to a dampened sheet of paper under great pressure through the rollers of an etching press. He then burnished the pastel into the surface of the print with great delicacy, so that the colour became a transparent tint over the original drawing.

One should attempt to work in a way that makes use of the particular qualities of pastel – it is no use trying to render fine detail with a stump of chalk. Work broadly and begin on a large scale with a sheet of paper big enough to allow the arm to move freely across the surface. Mistakes in the drawing can usually be brushed away with a hog's-hair brush. Take care not to destroy the grain of the paper when erasing parts of the drawing. It is the pronounced grain of the paper which anchors the particles of chalk to the surface. The simple, bold statement is usually the most successful; pastels which are overworked lose their 'bite' and feeling of spontaneity. Toned or tinted papers make an ideal base for pastel drawings. Watercolour papers can be tinted by using diluted gouache, which can be rubbed into the grain or the paper with a soft pad of cloth.

Oil pastels are quite different from chalk pastels; they are softer and more malleable. The resulting blending of one colour with another can give a very rich effect. Oil pastels can be scraped with the sharp edge of a blade, which gives the drawing a kind of sculptural quality. The resistance of the medium make it most suitable for strong, expressive statements.

Above: Types of chalks and pastels: Pastels are manufactured in varying degrees of hardness. **1** Castell Polychromos **2** Inscribe soft pencil **3** Guitar oil pastel **4** Pentel oil pastel **5** chalk pastel.

Below: Dancer II: pencil and coloured crayon on toned paper. The drawing relies on under-statement to lend emphasis to the delicacy of the subject.

Above: 1 Girl and Cat: Pastel The main drawing is taken almost to completion in a dark grey pastel softened with a sable brush and water. The chalk tones are modified by working over the grey with a purple chalk.

Above: 2 The darker tones begin to recede as other colours are added. The artist uses colour to establish the link between the cat in the bottom left hand corner, diagonally towards the girl's head in the top right hand corner.

A balance is achieved in terms of colour and tone. The colours are softened by being fused together with a torchon.

Right: Sketchbook study: William Turner
A rapid notation in pastel using a black chalk to reinforce to low horizon.

Fixing pastel drawings with a mouth spray

Fixing from the back with an aerosol spray. Hold the drawing at a distance and spray lightly.

Left: Grumbacher
This set of chalk pastels consists of 336 colours. It would normally be used by an artist who has chosen to specialize in pastel. A set of 12 colours is sufficient for most needs.

CHAPTER 3

PAINTING

WATERCOLOUR

THE fickle nuances, muted tones and hues of landscape are ideally conveyed in watercolour painting. No other medium offers the same range of atmospheric and luminous qualities. Through watercolour painters were released from the formal pretentiousness of 'Academy' painting. They were able to escape the confines of the studio and gain a more direct contact with nature. Thomas Gainsborough complained to his friend, William Jackson, that he was 'sick of portraits' and that he wanted to find some sweet village where he could paint 'landskips and enjoy the fag end of life in quietness and ease'.

Watercolour has always been subordinate to oil-painting. Even today it is much underrated as a legitimate means of expression. Watercolour painting is characteristically an 'English' medium, owing little to any European tradition. The qualities of watercolour are seen at their best in Turner's 'colour beginnings' and topographical studies. Since the end of the nineteenth century, however, watercolour has been widely adopted by amateur painters and this has resulted in its becoming subjected to all kinds of mannerisms and formulas. This is not to decry the fine tradition of watercolour painting among amateurs. Their

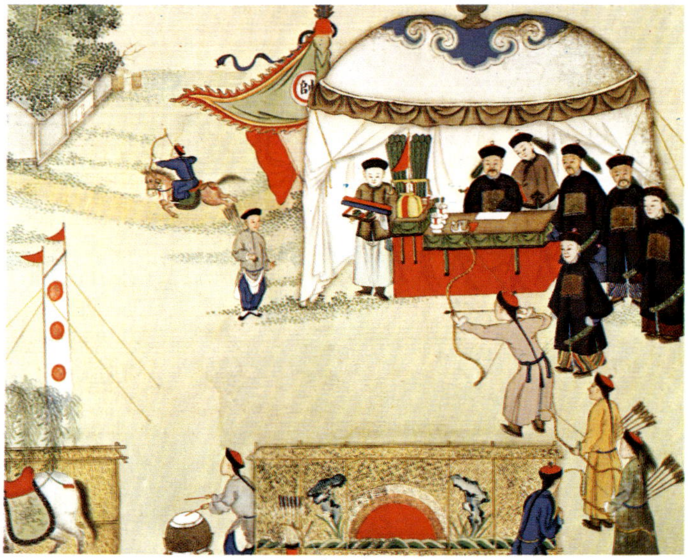

Above: Archers: Late 18th-century Chinese painting. This drawing produced on silk shows richness of colour, and ingenuity in the composition. A variety of textural marks are used.

Below left: The Indian village of Pomeioc 1585
An early record of American life drawn descriptively with a thick brush line and wash.

Bamboo brushes. The long tapering brushes favoured by Chinese artists are ideal for watercolour painting – especially when working with broad washes.

work is often far more perceptive than that to be found in many a gallery. But the most successful works are usually those that are produced spontaneously, that are not hide-bound by technical conventions or overworked to a degree where they become 'picturesque'. The essence of water-colour lies in the swiftness of the statement; it does not lend itself to the laborious modelling techniques of oil painting.

The English tradition in watercolour painting paralleled the Romantic revival among the great English poets. Tennyson, Wordsworth, Clare, Gray, Cowper and many others found inspiration in close contact with nature. Turner was first and foremost a watercolourist; when he used oil paints he tended to thin them down into transparent glazes, particularly in his seascapes. His conception demanded a greater lucidity than could be achieved with the usual paste-like consistency of oil-bound pigment. French painters marvelled at the English 'aquarellists' who exhibited at the Paris Salon of 1824. Corot described how, on seeing the watercolours of Bonington, he was transformed from an errand boy to a painter.

Above: Venice from the Giudecca: J. M. W. Turner This painting characterises Turner's mastery of the water-colour technique.

Below: *Superimposed washes in a single colour.* Tonal gradations can be achieved by laying washes of the same strength on top of one another. Each wash must be allowed to dry before the next is laid.

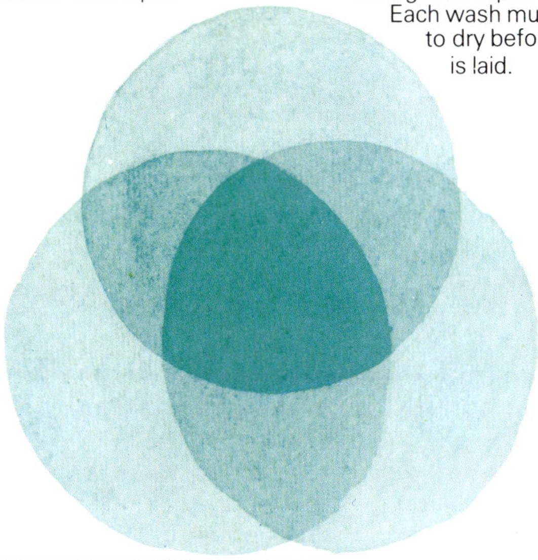

Left: The White House, Chelsea: Thomas Girtin
Girtin was one of the first English artists to concentrate on watercolour. In this painting he used just five colours, overlaid to produce a painting of depth and richness of colour.

Opposite below: *Gouache colours* The range of commercially available gouache is indicated by these colour charts. Gouache is also referred to as 'designers' colour' or 'opaque watercolour'. The colours come in the form of either tubes or cakes. Gouache is extensively used for commercial illustration work because the opacity of the paint is well suited to being reproduced.

Many painters, including Turner, were indebted to the work of John Robert Cozens, who, in addition to making the usual topographical studies of 'The Grand Tour', produced numerous watercolour sketches of desolate and barren landscapes. Constable described his paintings as 'all poetry' and Cozens himself as 'the greatest genius that ever touched landscape'. As a teacher, Cozens did not follow the convention of instructing his pupils to copy either his own work or that of the great masters. Believing that such methods served only to weaken his students' powers of invention, he encouraged them to experiment with technique, suggesting that they should develop landscapes from 'blots' of colour.

The development of landscape watercolour painting in England was an important factor in the formation of England's only recognizable 'school' of painting, the Norwich school, founded by John Crome and later joined by John Sell Cotman. These two, together with their children and friends, formed a society whose common aim was to work directly from nature. Working in East Anglia, where flat planes and large expanses of sky produce striking qualities of light, they tended to use natural colour values, rather than the colour schemes of the Italian schools which had such a dominating influence on painters working elsewhere. Cotman's skill as a watercolourist has never been surpassed, but there are those who feel that technique sometimes replaced real personal expression in his work.

After Blake and Palmer, watercolour became established as the medium most suited to recording various aspects of the English scene. The tradition was maintained by Paul Nash and, later, his students, Edward Bawden and Eric Ravillious. All three were war artists during the Second World War. They found in watercolour a natural choice in their approach to landscape painting. In the United States a tradition in watercolour painting was established by such artists as Winslow Homer, Thomas Eakins and, more recently, Andrew Wyeth.

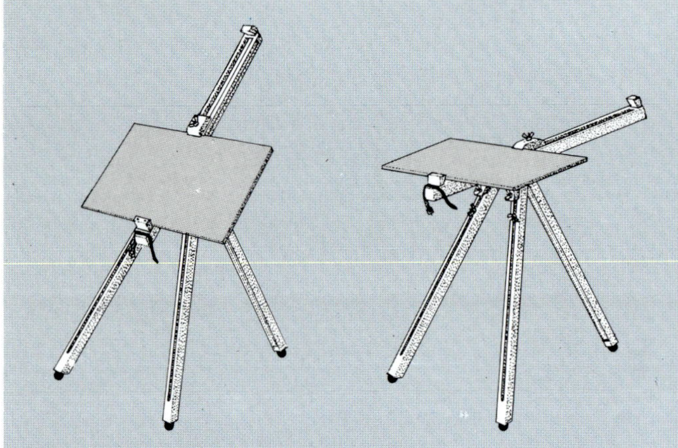

A collapsible easel which is light and easy to carry is useful for watercolour painting when set horizontally.

The watercolour paintings of Paul Cézanne are worthy of special consideration, and I would recommend any serious student to study them, even in reproduction. Even Cézanne's most inconclusive watercolours seem to possess the quality of completeness. It was through watercolour that Cézanne discovered the use of coloured patches which characterized his later work. Using a limited number of washes, he would overlay blue and green and perhaps yellow ochre in various strengths to give his paintings the quality of vibrant modulation. The nearest points of each object were left white, not as highlights, but to suggest volume. This was in line with the dictum that nature was modelled on the sphere, the cylinder and the cone.

Left: Stan Smith: Two Figures. The underpainting was still damp when the artist developed strong highlight areas on top of it.

GOUACHE

Gouache is sometimes called 'body colour'. Like watercolour, it is bound in gum arabic and is soluble in water. It is characterized by a rich, matt, opaque surface which lacks the transparency of watercolour and the gloss of oil paint. It is a fine medium for architectural subjects, or for figures in interiors, since it lends itself to fine detail. Historically it was used primarily for manuscripts, although in the seventeenth century it became more widely used as a medium for painting by Italian and Dutch artists, including Zuccarelli and Van Dyck. In the eighteenth century, Paul Sandby used both watercolour and gouache extensively. Toulouse Lautrec produced some of his finest café paintings using gouache on scraps of brown paper and card. Edouard Vuillard painted his evocative, atmospheric interiors using a dry-brush technique. Among contemporary artists, the gouache paintings by Keith Vaughan, Ceri Richards and Graham Sutherland are outstanding.

Gouache is an ideal medium for recording the changing conditions of light in landscape painting. It dries quite rapidly and with a limited palette one can continually modify tones in such a way that the right balance is achieved. The opacity of the colour makes it possible to re-work certain passages of the painting in a way that is not possible in watercolour.

Above: The colour is diluted almost to the consistency of watercolour to register the main forms in the landscape view.

Right: Colours in the middle-distance are intensified to concentrate attention on that part of the composition.

Left and right: The various parts of the painting begin to work together. The detail in the foreground is understated in order to focus on the valley and distant hills.

The darker tones of the trees provide a visual link from the foreground to the distance. White body colour is added to the clouds and horizon.

USING GUM ARABIC

Gum arabic is the medium that binds the pigments in watercolour. A dilute form is also very useful. It adds richness and texture to watercolour and, because it acts as a kind of varnish, keeps the colours very bright. The artist started by painting the hedge with pure watercolour. He then mixed dilute gum arabic with the paint and you can see how much denser the colour is. He added more texture to the foliage of the tree by sprinkling it with water, creating splattered areas of lighter colour which suggest the pattern of light on leaves. He then blotted the wet area and more of the colour lifted off.

The landscape of Italy, and the region of Tuscany in particular, has long been favoured by artists. A small farmhouse nestling between cypress trees on a hillside, provides the subject for this painting. The artist must first select his viewpoint, and this might mean walking around the subject to view it from different angles and different levels. The farmhouse itself provides the main interest, and everything in the painting appears to radiate from it. The pink stucco of the building contrasts with the olive green colour of the surrounding trees and vines. The tall verticals of the cypress trees draw attention to the centre of the composition.

Above: 1 The landscape is drawn lightly in a soft pencil. Washes of colour are added very sparingly with a No.6 sable hair brush.

Below: 2 The details such as windows and contours are more sharply defined with a No.3 sable hair brush. Washes are overlaid in certain areas with a broader brush to bring the tones closer together.

A harmony is established in terms of the colour relationships and in the related parts of the composition.

OIL/TEMPERA

ARTISTS' colourmen manufacture two grades of oil paint – 'Artists' quality, which has a high degree of permanence, and a 'Student' grade, which is less permanent. Apart from tubes, the most economical way to buy oil paint is in 1lb tins.

Anyone who has witnessed the cleaning of an old oil painting will appreciate how age and pollutants can deaden colour values. Some pigments, especially blues, tend to be fugitive; earth colours are the most permanent.

There are many different approaches to oil painting. Some artists build up a painting over a period of time, applying layers of paint on top of one another. Other artists like to complete a painting in a single session in order to give the work immediacy and spontaneity. After the art dealer, Ambroise Vollard, had sat for Cézanne over a period of many months, he enquired of the artist as to the progress of the painting. After careful consideration, Cézanne said that he thought that he had got the shirt front just about right! When one compares the small oil sketches made directly from nature by Constable and Turner with the large-scale works derived from the sketches in the studio, one sees both losses and gains. Something of the freshness of the preliminary sketches is lost in the larger canvases. On the other hand, the studio paintings impress by their sheer grandeur of scale and dramatic composition.

Most painters start to work either by making an under-drawing in charcoal on the surface of the canvas or by under-painting in a single colour. Those who are intimidated by an expanse of white, empty canvas might consider staining the surface with dilute oil colour – perhaps an ochre or grey. The stain should be gently rubbed into the weave of the canvas and should be sufficiently thinned down so that it does not clog the tooth of the canvas.

Once the under-drawing or under-painting is completed, one can begin to lay in larger areas of colour. The first hour or so, when the painting begins to take shape, is often the most stimulating. It can also be the most critical stage, for one has to decide how far to develop a painting without overworking or obliterating too much of the early stages. A kind of battle ensues, and one decides to leave parts of the under-painting exposed while painting out other passages. There is a point to be reached where there is an interaction between flat areas of colour and descriptive brushwork drawing. At the point when the balance seems to work, the painting might be considered to be 'finished'.

Every artist at some time goes beyond the point and realizes that he has gone too far to reclaim what he has lost. We can only learn by experience to know when to stop.

Above: Christina's world: Andrew Wyeth
Wyeth is best known for his tempera paintings. The luminosity of the painting and the fine working of the detail is offset by the pale wash of the sky which reveals the gesso ground.

Left: Chair, coats, mirror, knotted curtain: David Tindle
Pure egg tempera was used. In many parts of the painting 30 or 40 washes were laid over one another with cross-hatching, stippling and other forms of texture applied as well.

TEMPERA

Painting in tempera requires a little more organization than working with oils. Tempera dries quickly and brushes need to be rinsed frequently in warm water. Glazing with tempera can be very rewarding. Layers of transparent colour can be built up quite quickly. Dry brush working can also be very effective. The brush takes up paint, most of which is put down on scrap paper, leaving the brush 'starved' of colour. Part of the paint surface can be scraped away with the edge of a blade to reveal the gesso ground and then repainted with a different, transparent glaze of colour so that the scraped texture shows through. The surface of a tempera painting can be fine, but also sculptural, as layers of paint are scraped away and reworked.

1 A wash of cobalt blue laid over yellow ochre.

2 Two colours overlaid produce other variations.

3 The kinetic effect of cross-hatched lines in white, umber and white/ochre.

4 The effect of scraping back the painting with a palette knife and dragging paint across the surface.

5 Lines scratched into opaque colour and additional washes laid over the surface.

6 Applying paint with a sponge produces a stippled effect.

7 Paint applied with a palette knife and glazed over with cadmium yellow.

8 Colours spattered widely wet-on-wet on a warm coloured ground.

Above: This typical Quattrocento (15th century) triptych is painted in many layers of tempera. The luminosity derives from an underlay of pure white gesso.

PAINTING A PORTRAIT

The features of the model are sharply defined when seen against the plain background of a white wall in the studio. A three-quarter view was selected by the artist standing at an easel 6 feet/2 metres distant. The model usually rests at half hour intervals so that the position of arms and hands needs to be marked with chalk. All the materials are within easy reach on a painting table.

Above: 1 The main features of the model are first drawn in lightly with a stick of charcoal.

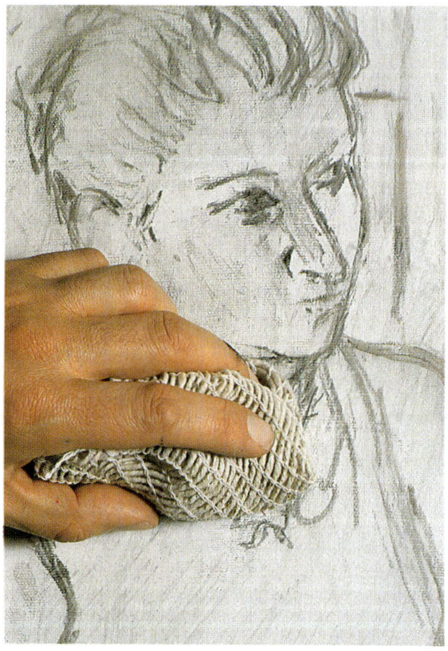

Above: 2 Charcoal tends to make colour dirty, so that the surface is brushed lightly with a cloth leaving a faint image of the drawing as a guide.

Above: 3 The contours are painted in a single colour – preferably a mid-tone.

Above: 4 Washes of the same colour are laid in to establish the light and dark areas of the painting.

Above: 5 Flesh tones are added and the dark Prussian blue of the sweater painted in, leaving some of the under-drawing exposed.

Above: 6 The various planes of the head are restated using a smaller brush.

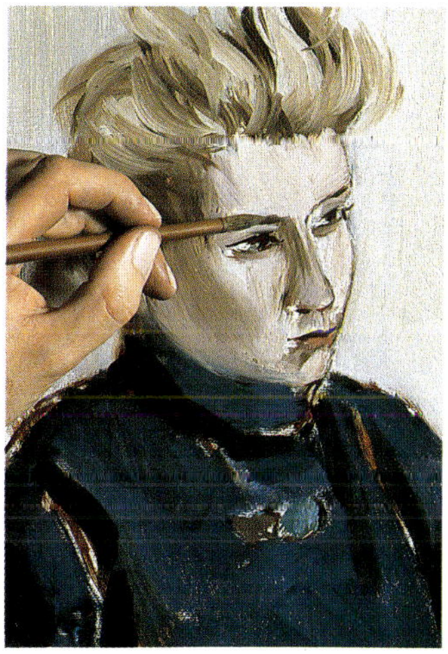

Above: 8 A bamboo brush with a fine tip is useful for features such as eyes, nose and mouth.

Right: 7 A hogshair brush is used to define the modelling of the head.

The completed painting. Part of the underdrawing is left exposed – the sitting for this study lasted approximately 1½ hours.

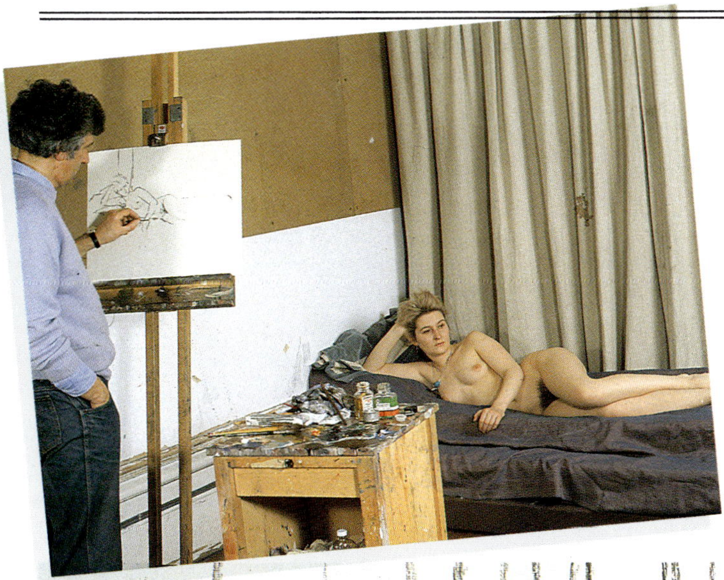

FIGURE STUDY

In posing the model, it is necessary to ensure that the posture is sufficiently comfortable to be maintained for long periods of time. The background should be fairly simple; in order to concentrate attention on the model without undue interference from intrusive objects such as tables and chairs. Depending on the season and the time of day, the light will be constantly changing, and one must learn to accommodate such changes as part of the process of painting.

Above: 1 The main forms are drawn on canvas with charcoal.

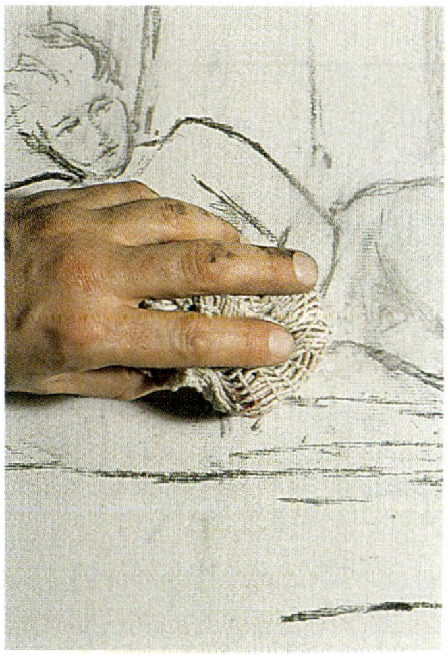

Above: 2 The surface is dusted in preparation for painting.

Above: 3 Drawing begins in a single colour and the main parts of the composition are firmly established.

Above: 4 Thin turpentine washes are applied to determine the main areas of tone.

Above: 5 Washes of colour are applied sparingly to the figure and background curtain. The under-drawing remains visible in parts.

Above: 6 The tones become more unified at this stage of the painting.

Above: 7 The colour is applied more solidly using linseed oil rather than turpentine.

Right: 8 Details in the drawing are painted with a finer sable brush.

The painting was completed in a single sitting of about 1 hour.

Left: Sofa: Terence Millington
Thin washes of acrylic paint were used in this painting on rough watercolour paper. A film of polyurethane varnish was applied over the top of the watercolour and wiped away leaving a soft brown tone over the whole surface.

Above: Girl lying in a hammock: Leonard Rosoman
The painting was built up gradually with glazes of acrylic on a prepared wooden panel.

ACRYLICS

ACRYLIC paints are being used increasingly by artists who previously worked in oil paint. This is surprising, since the essential substance of the colour is closer to tempera or gouache than to oil. The matt body of the colour is not really suited to the kind of heavy impasto modelling that can be obtained with oil paint. Abstract painters like the covering capacity of acrylic and the smooth, even finish that can be obtained when working on large canvases.

One of the most attractive features of acrylics is that transparent washes of colour can be laid over one another. Glazes of colour are made by thinning the paint with either water or a special acrylic medium. When undiluted, acrylic paint can be quite stiff, depending on the colour used. To cover a canvas with large flat areas of colour which do not reveal brushmarks, several coats may be required. Alternatively, a substance called 'water tension breaker' can be added to the paint to give it a more even flow.

With practice one learns to combine transparent and opaque colours to produce a variety of qualities in a painting. The fact that acrylic paint is fast-drying makes it an ideal medium for painting landscape directly from nature. Colours do tend to darken as they dry and one might need to compensate for this when mixing them. Fine detail is possible and it is interesting to fuse linear qualities with broad expanses of semi-transparent colour. Much depends, of course, on the subject you are painting. An atmospheric seascape, for instance, may require only a basic linear under-painting, whereas a portrait or figure study will require more structured analysis.

Above left: 1 The simple elements of the landscape are painted in green and umber with a hogshair brush.

Above: 2 Thin washes of other colours complete the composition.

Above: 3 The mood and atmosphere of the painting are determined by modified colours in the sky and foreground.

The completed painting shows colour and tone working together.

Above: 1 The artist chose to paint this view because he was fascinated by the way the hedge enclosed and revealed the landscape beyond.

Working outside presents its own particular problems. It will be necessary to carry with you all the equipment that you might need, including brushes, palette knives, paints, canvas or board, painting mediums – linseed oil and turpentine, and plenty of clean rag. Additionally, you will need a collapsible sketching easel, or some other means of support for the canvas. Selecting the viewpoint may also be difficult in a vast expanse of landscape. You can make a framing device by cutting a rectangular window from a piece of card. This will help to separate out parts of the landscape and to view things in isolation. The colours you squeeze out of tubes will also seem much brighter in daylight.

Left: 2 The artist works outdoors on the subject. Even if you prefer to work in the studio you should occasionally paint from nature because it is a unique experience. The artist makes the initial drawing directly on to the canvas with charcoal.

Right: 3 Charcoal is a flexible medium, capable of creating a sinuous line. It is easily erased and therefore easily corrected, a great advantage when an artist is evolving a composition on the canvas. Having decided on the outlines of the composition the artist knocks it back with a cloth.

Right: 4 Having removed the surface particles from the charcoal drawing, the artist traces over the faint, remaining lines with thinned black paint. He starts to block in colour, laying in the sky with a mixture of cobalt blue and white.

Above: 5 When working with a painting knife it is best to work *alla prima*, that is, laying on all the pigments in one session and in one layer.

Left: 6 The artist uses a knife because he is anxious to complete the painting at one sitting. With a pallet knife a painting can be built up very quickly indeed.

Right: 7 In the detail we see thick, glossy paint laid on *alla prima*. In some places the canvas shines through the viridian, a particularly translucent colour: in others, different greens have been smeared together.

Above: 8 It is possible to work in quite a detailed way with a painting knife – it is not necessarily a crude instrument. The artist works colour between the bars of the gate, using small dabs of colour laid on with the very tip of the blade. Even the fairly small bars of the gate are rendered with the knife.

Above: 9 The details illustrated in Steps 7 and 8 are shown above in the context of the whole painting. The artist has moved from one part of the painting to the other, picking up colours and moving them across the canvas. These stray bits of colour link the various elements of the painting. The painting illustrates how different the surfaces created by a knife can be. There are small, subtly modulated areas of tone in the sky contrasted with exciting, dragged colour in the foliage.

Left: 10 The artist establishes a small area of local colour on the distant hills using a mixture of yellow ochre, white and cadmium yellow. The artist uses small strokes of the knife to lay in colour in this area.

The finished picture shows how the gateway frames the hills, and helps to create a feeling of distance.

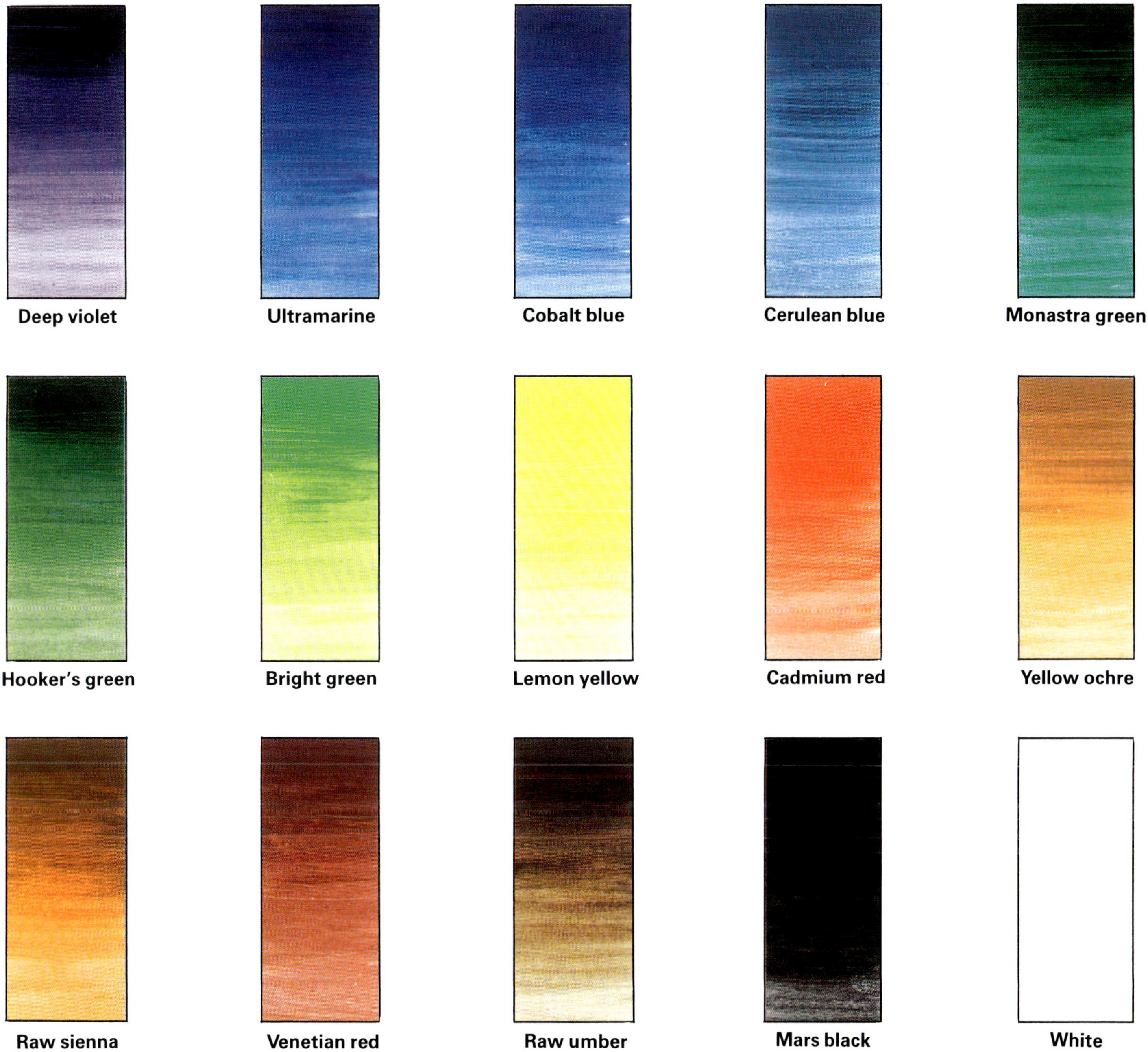

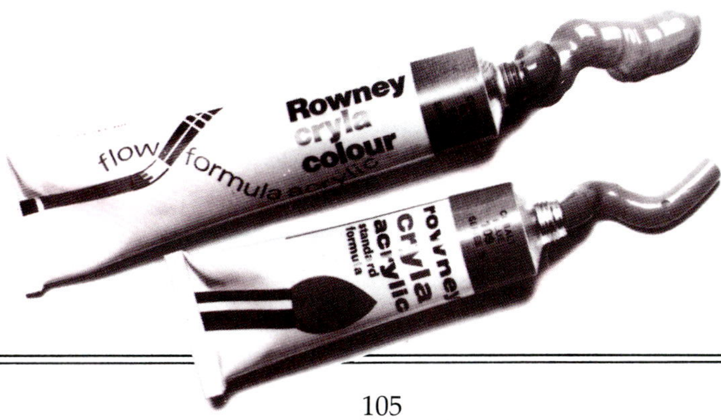

Left: Rowneys Flow Formula paint is more liquid than other acrylics but retains the same density.

CHAPTER 4

PRESENTATION

Above left to right: Common mouldings (moldings)
1 Box
2 Reverse slope
3 Flat
4 Half-round

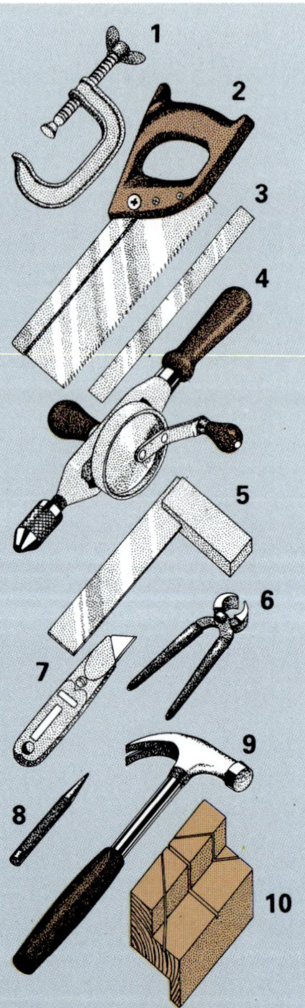

Tools for framing
1 G-Clamp **2** Tenon saw
3 Metal ruler **4** Hand drill
5 Tri-square (try-square)
6 Pincers **7** Stanley knife (craft knife) **8** Punch
9 Claw hammer
10 Mitre saw guide

MOUNTING/FRAMING/ EXHIBITING

The mounting and presentation of paintings and drawings is a craft in its own right. Every work of art needs a separator of some kind. It is essential to isolate a drawing or painting from its immediate surroundings, so that it can be seen clearly at full value. Watercolours, gouaches and drawings require window mounts with generous borders. White or cream or various coloured mounts can be matched against the painting. More often than not a neutral tint makes a better separator than a strong colour, though in some instances a richly coloured mount can enhance the work. Window mounts also serve the more practical purpose of keeping the painting or drawing from coming into contact with the glass. The window shape cut from the card should be set above centre so that the bottom margin is proportionally larger than the remaining sides. There are a number of mount-cutters which are easy to use currently on the market – they have an adjustable blade which can be angled to cut a bevelled mount. If possible, always use an acid-free tape for fixing your drawing or painting to the mount. This prevents the work from becoming discoloured at a later date. Acid-free mounting board is also recommended, but it can be very expensive.

Framing any painting needs careful consideration; an overly decorative gilt mounting, for instance, may be too overbearing on a simple landscape painting. Most professional framers will allow you to test sample mitred corners of different types of moulding against your own painting to see whether any of them is suitable. Prints and drawings often work quite well in a stainless-steel or self-assembly aluminium frame. Charcoal drawings and pencil drawings work best in a simple half-round or box wooden moulding. Watercolours, if properly mounted, can be enhanced by

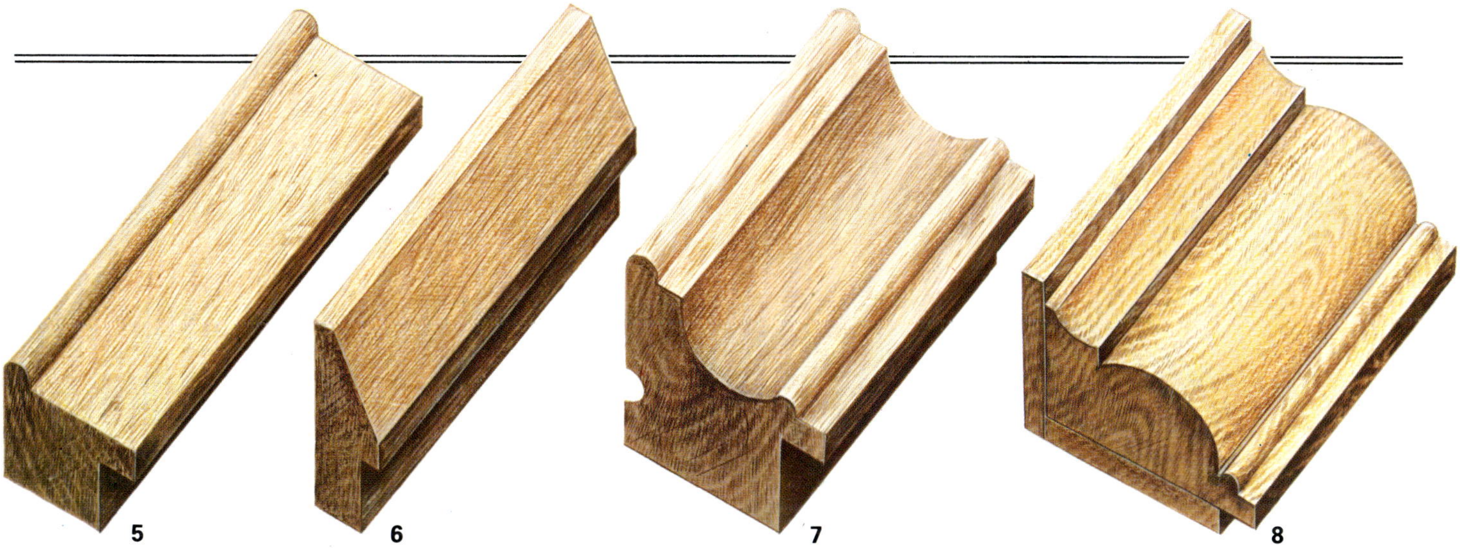

Above left to right:
5 Raised bead and flat
6 Box
7 Spoon
8 Composite made from planed timber and architrave moulding

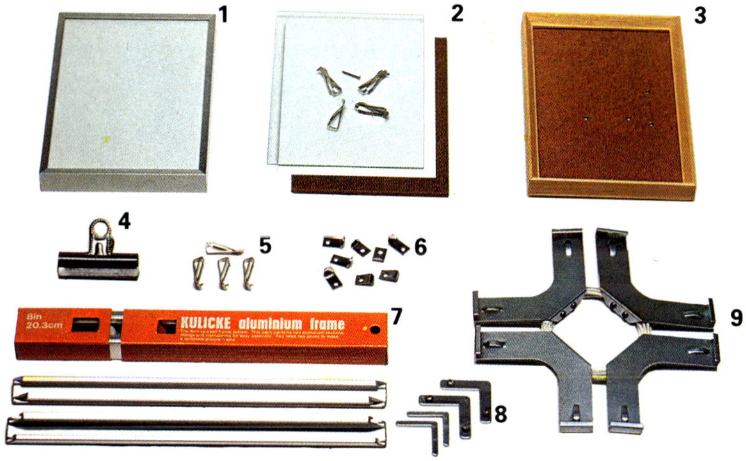

Above: *Ready-made frames and clips* **1** Emo interchangeable metal frame **2** Emo framers' pack, containing a piece of glass, a piece of fibreboard and a number of small clips **3** Ready-made frame **4, 5** and **6** Bulldog, spring and mirror clips **7** and **8** Kulicke and Daler metal frame kits **9** Hang-it frame kit.

narrow half-round gilt or silver wooden frames. Larger mouldings are best for oil and acrylic paintings. Quite often a fabric slip set inside the rebate can act as an additional separator between the frame and the painting.

An artist is not always the best judge of how his work is best framed; he is often so close to the work that he finds it hard to make the right choice. For this reason I would suggest that much can be gained by seeking a second opinion, either from a frame-maker or from a fellow-artist whose opinion you value. Remember that the main purpose of a frame is to act as a separator: it is better to be formal than flamboyant.

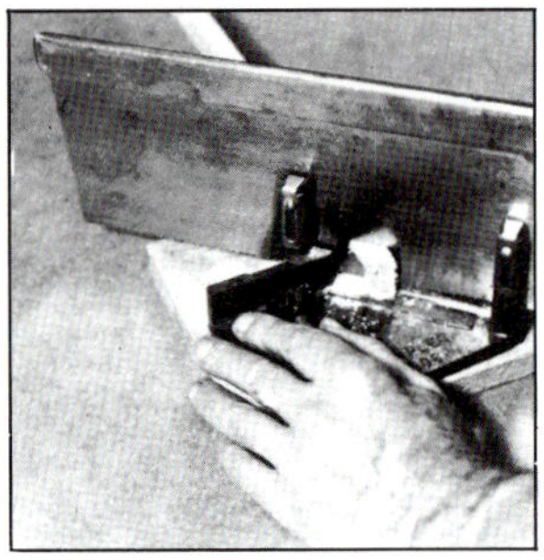

Cutting a mitre **1** Place a length of moulding in the mitre clamp. Use pieces of wood either side to avoid bruising. Saw off angle.

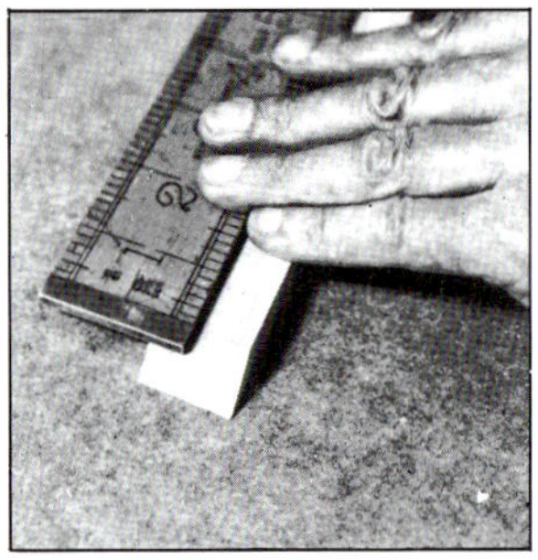

2 Measure the length from the inside edge of the mitre.

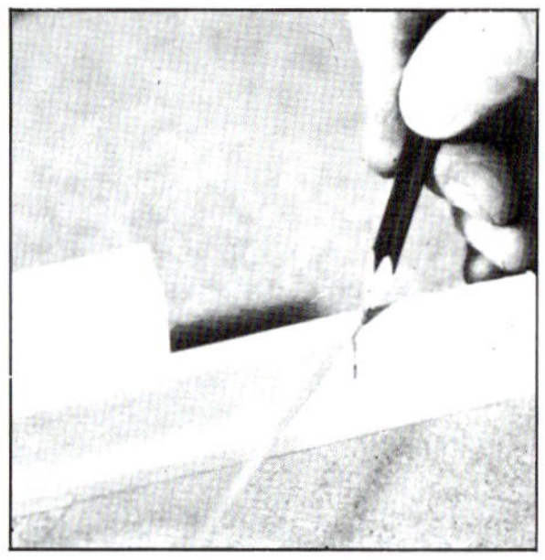

3 Mark the next cut at an angle of 45 degrees using a set square.

4 Make sure that the saw cuts exactly on the waste side of the mark and repeat for other sides of the frame.

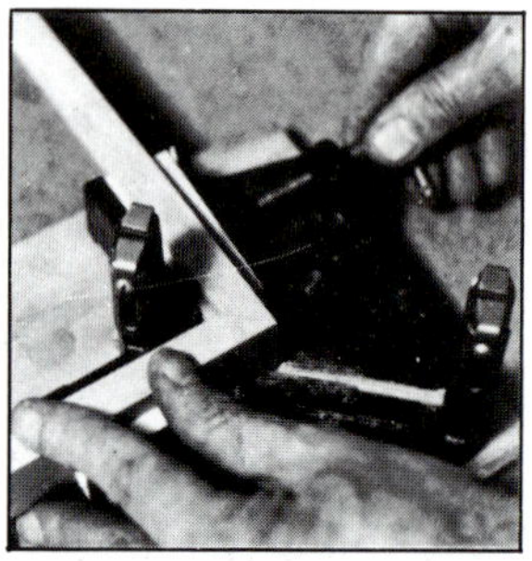

Assembling a frame **1** The corners are assembled in the mitre clamp – check the join carefully.

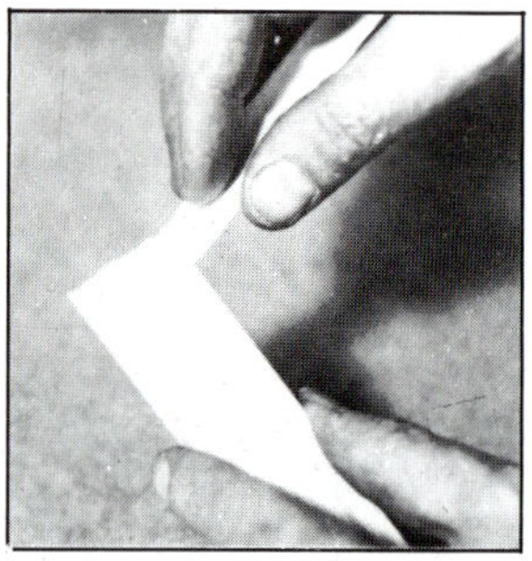

2 Release the clamp and spread glue on to the left hand piece of the mitred-face.

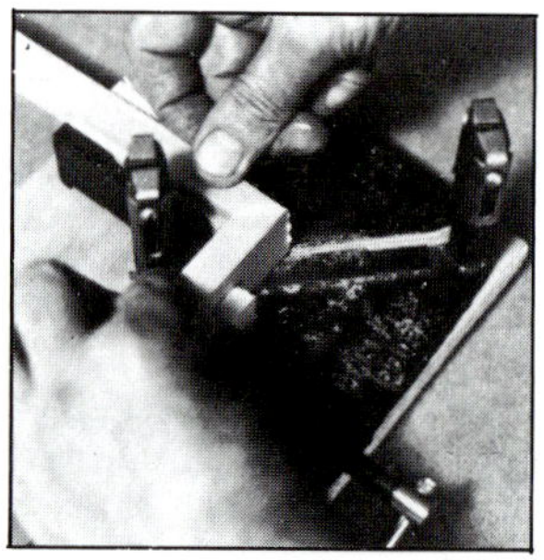

3 Replace in the clamp pressing firmly against the other piece. Tighten in the clamp.

4 Shallow recesses are drilled in the side of the moulding for panel pins.

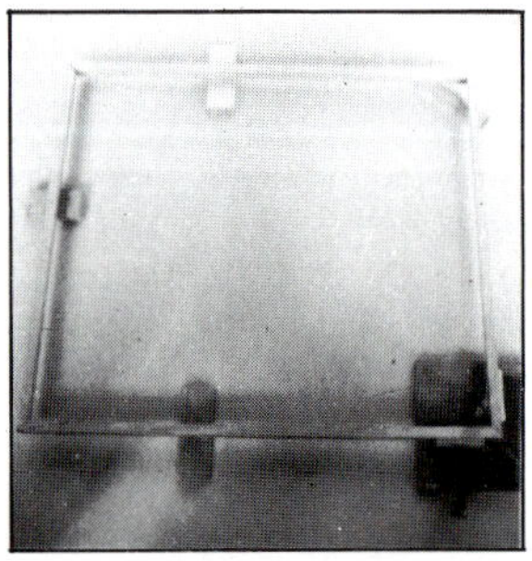

5 Gently knock the panel pins into the moulding at an angle.
6 Repeat on other sides and join the two 'L' shapes together.

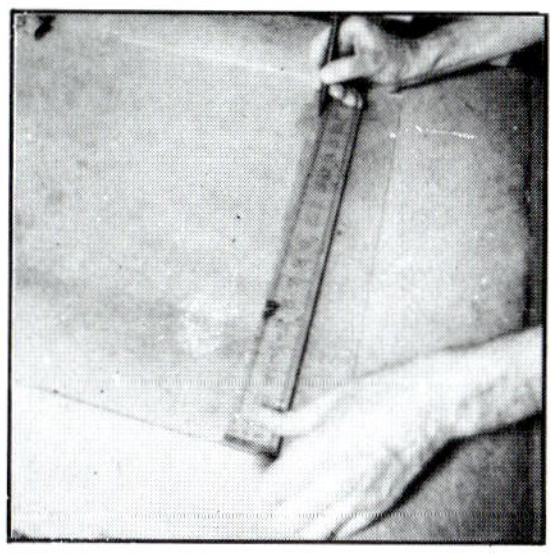

Cutting glass **1** Mark the first cut with a ruler and felt pen.

2 Using a straight edge and set square.

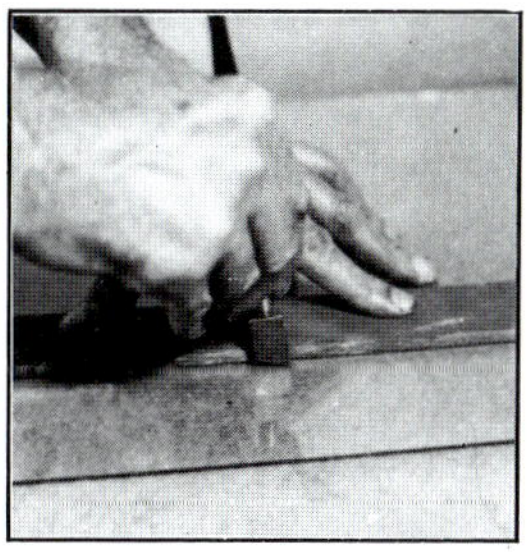

3 On the far edge of the glass draw the cutter down the surface – pressing firmly but not too hard.

4 Tap the glass gently to open the cut, and snap the glass.

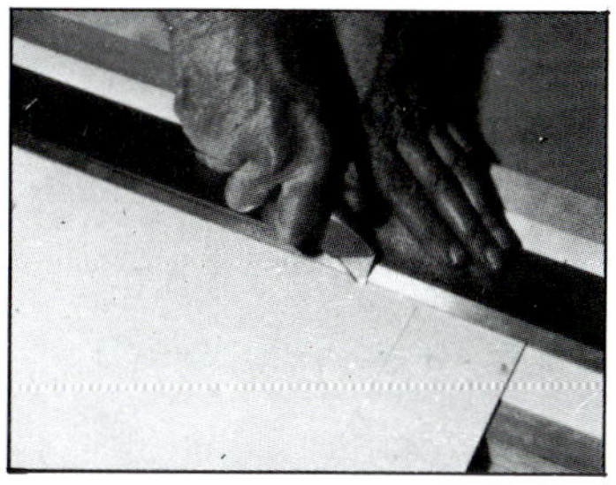

Cutting a window mount **1** The corners of the area to be cut are marked with pin pricks. Cut from one corner to the other holding the knife at an angle of 45 degrees.

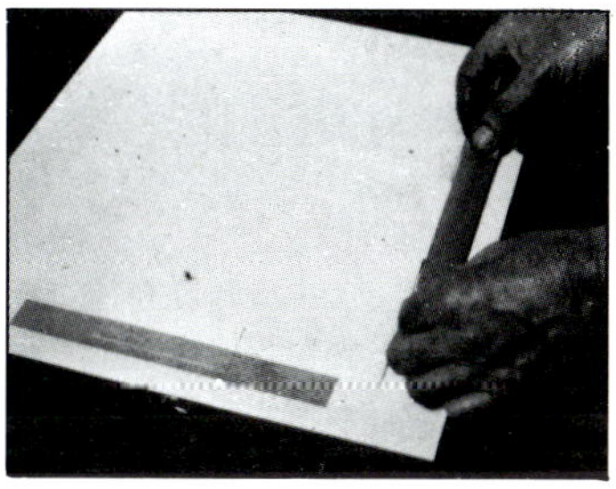

2 Attach the painting to the mount with (acid-free) adhesive tape.

3 The image as it appears in the window mount showing the bevelled edge.

4 Notice the slight border around the edges allowing space at the bottom for the artist's signature.

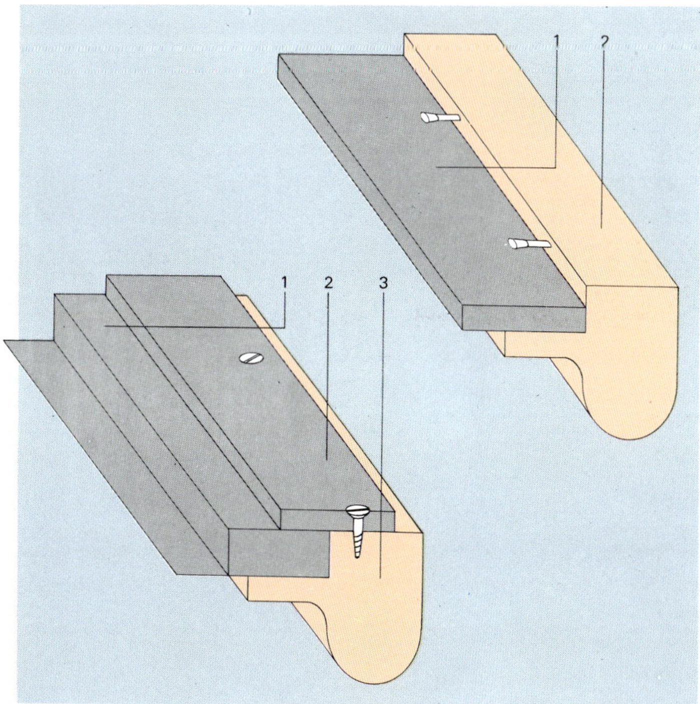

Left: *Types of frame.*

Left: Securing with brads a small picture can be held in the frame **1** and secured with brads tapped into the frame **2.**

Left: Using battens. Larger canvases **1** are held in the frame with battens **2** and secured with screws **3.**

Mounts and Mounting

It is important to differentiate clearly between the mount – the 'window' which is placed upon the artwork – and the backing card or board onto which the artwork is stuck before the process begins. Confusion arises because this backing is often referred to as the mount. The means by which the artwork is stuck to this backing is also referred to as 'mounting'. This section discusses the general principles of mounts and mounting.

THE BREATHING SPACE

Many artpieces are mounted as well as framed. In other words, the picture does not make direct contact with the frame but is surrounded by a wide margin which separates the picture from the frame. This is the mount. It is the 'breathing space' between the picture content and the frame itself.

There are no rigid rules governing whether you should or should not have a mount within your frame but, as a basic guideline, consider the artpiece itself: does it, for instance, contain large areas of empty space in its composition, as in the case of a line drawing on a plain white background? This sort of picture would look effective with only a small amount of border, or possibly with none at all. On the other hand, a more crowded picture would benefit from a substantial border of space between the image and the frame.

The mount should be chosen before the frame, because it is the mount that comes next to the artpiece. A great deal of mystery has been attached to the 'proportions' of the mount – the amount of space which should be left at the bottom, sides and top of the image. In fact, the choice is personal and there is nothing magical about the measurements.

Above: Mount widths.
The width of the mount has an immediate effect on the framed picture as a whole. If the mount is too small, it can give the picture a cramped and restricted look. An equal all-round width works well with some images. If the mount is large in comparison with the picture, it is usually better if the picture 'sits' high up in the frame – make sure the mount margin at the bottom of the picture is deeper than that of the other three sides.

Opposite: Choosing a colour
The landscape shown here is painted in muted, earthy colours. With a picture like this, it is usually advisable to choose a colour that harmonizes with the subject. The light beige mount makes the picture look darker; the dull olive green immediately picks out the green tones in the composition; black emphasizes the linear content. Sometimes a mount of an unrelated colour works: the rich magenta contrasts attractively with the greens and browns in the picture.

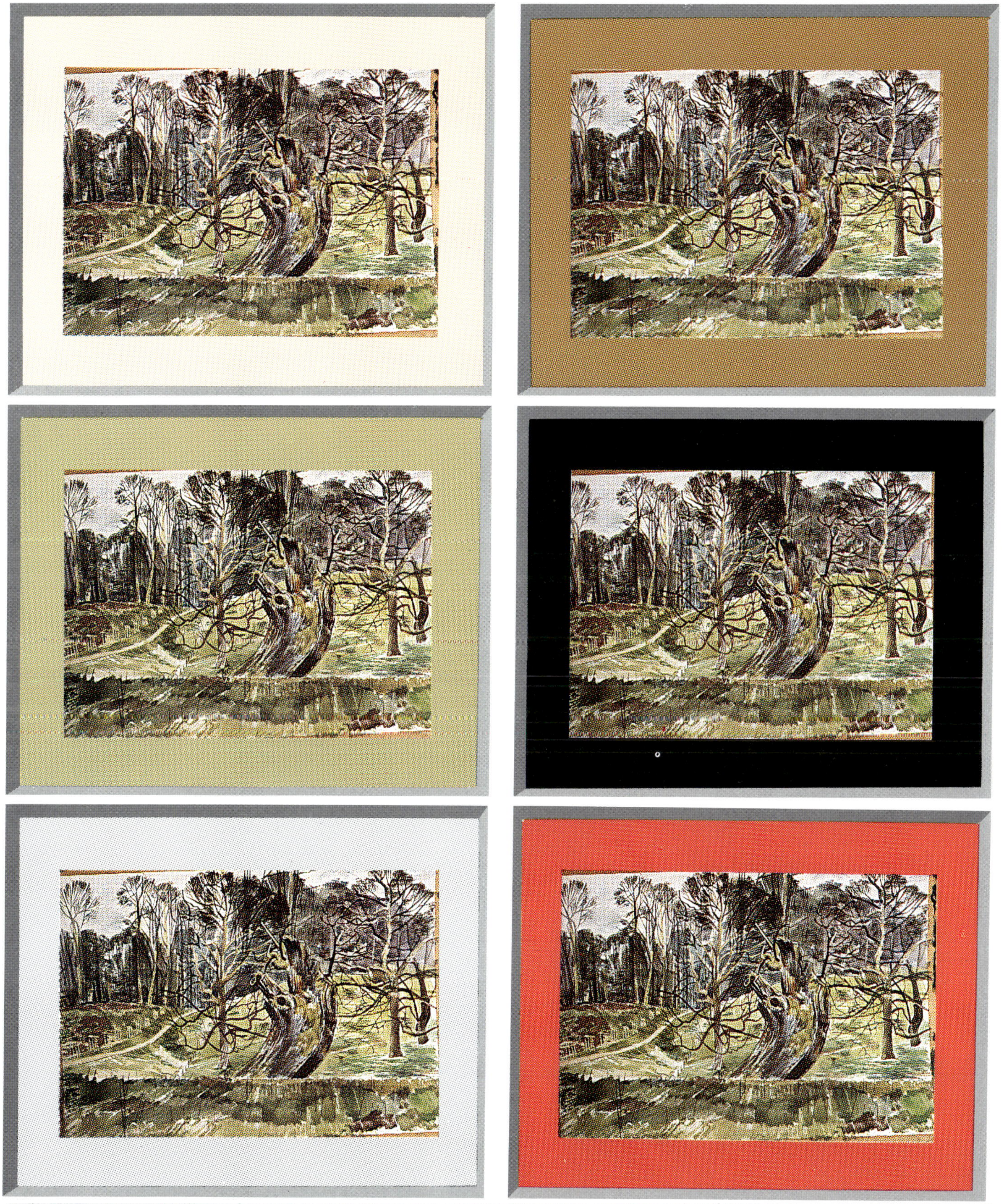

The proportion of the mount should not compete with the proportions of the artwork; that is, a big picture does not necessarily need a wide mount and a small picture does not always benefit from having a narrow mount. Generally speaking, a small picture is much improved by a wide mount and a grand-looking frame. Do not follow this principle slavishly or you will end up with a postage-stamp-size picture in the middle of a poster-size mount! There are some exceptions. Small photographs can sometimes look good with narrow mounts. A flamboyant modern print can benefit from a wide mount. The result is usually more effective if you avoid giving the visual impression that you have used exactly the same area for the mount as for the artpiece.

There is one important visual illusion which needs to be considered. If the width of space around an artpiece is equal, then the bottom will appear smaller than the other margins. Therefore, an impression of symmetry is best produced by having the space at the bottom a little larger than the other margins – between 6mm (¼in) and 18mm (¾in) is enough in most cases, depending on the size of the artpiece.

Above and left: A picture in bright, expressionistic colours poses a very different problem. The mount generally should be as strong and bright as the colours contained in the painting. The red, blue, yellow, pink and mauve mounts all emphasize these particular colours in the portrait. The lime green provides a contrast; the white mount is effective because it picks out the background of the picture, giving a light, spacious feel.

BOUGHT FRAMES AND MOULDINGS

A FINE, grained frame with a raised inner edge stands complete at the top right of this selection. The group of grained woods and veneers illustrates the range of frames and mouldings available. At the bottom left-hand corner are two types of frame for an oval picture, including a gold slip oval that would enhance a particularly treasured period miniature. A more formal style of room cries out for the more formal, polished frames that are typical of those grouped together here. Among the narrower frames is an elegant tortoiseshell and gold, two sides of which, are illustrated at the top left. Next to it is a corner piece in antique walnut veneer. Some solid and grand frames lie across the centre of the group, including one with fan-shaped wooden inlays. Take care when choosing frames of this sort – consideration should be given not only to the type of picture to be framed, but also to the suitability of the frame to the environment where the picture will hang.

COLOURFUL PAINT FINISHES

SOME highly decorative paint finishes are featured in this group of mouldings. All ready-cut frames, they combine a traditional period flavour with modern experimental finishes. The yellow-marbled frame across the centre is frankly faked. Yet the result is a tasteful version of a traditional marbling technique, even though the colours are chosen to blend well with a modern interior. It contrasts strongly with the simple green and turquoise ovals that lie next to it in the group. To their bottom right is a series of specimens including a 'faux' or 'made' (imitation) malachite, and two elegant and narrow samples finished in stippled red and sponged blue. At the extreme top left of the whole group is a marbled dark blue frame, followed by frames sporting a variety of decorative finishes, including two rectangles with painted motifs and decoration over white and green stippled backgrounds.

APPENDIX

GLOSSARY

A

Acrylic A polymer based on synthetic resin. Acrylic paint, which is pigment dispersed in acrylic emulsion, dries to a tough, non-toxic flexible film. Acrylic emulsion is used principally as a painting medium, but also as a varnish for acrylic paintings.

Alizarin A synthetic coal-tar dye used in the manufacture of pigments.

Alla prima A method by which a passage of painting is completed with wet pigment in one session.

Amyl acetate Obtained from alcohol, and used as a solvent for some synthetic resins.

Aqueous Applied to painting, refers to media and pigments soluble or suspensible in water.

B

Binder In painting, any medium of some liquidity which forms a paint when mixed with powder pigment.

Bitumen A tarry substance formerly used as an oil colour. Now obsolete in painting because of its tendency to crack and darken.

Bloom A white discolouration on the surface of varnish.

Bole A clay, often red, used as a preparatory undercoat for gold leaf.

Bright A flat brush.

Burnishers Tools used for polishing surfaces, such as gold leaf and etching plates.

C

Cadmiums In painting, brilliant and permanent pigments prepared from cadmium sulphate.

Canada balsam See Venice turpentine.

Casein The protein of milk, produced by separation of curd from sour skimmed milk. Dried and mixed with acid, it is used as an adhesive or paint-binder.

Catalysis Effect produced by substance which causes a chemical change in other bodies while remaining itself unchanged. Thus egg will emulsify water and oil by acting as a catalyst.

Chamfer A symmetrical bevel cut in a right-angled edge or corner.

Chiaroscuro Pronounced quality of light and shade in painting.

Chinese ink See Indian ink.

Chinese white See Zinc white.

Cobalt A metal resembling nickel from which a range of pigments is made.

Copal A resin made from fossil trees, used as a varnish and in paint media.

Cover The capacity of a pigment to obscure an underlying surface. Alternatively, its capacity to extend by given volume over a surface.

D

Damar A coniferous resin used as a varnish, and sometimes as part of a mixed medium.

Distemper A water-soluble paint using egg-yolk or glue-size as a binder. Used mostly for flat indoor wall decoration.

Drypoint Method of working directly into a metal engraving surface with a point.

E

Earth colours Pigments made from inert minerals, such as ochres, siennas and umbers.

Efflorescence Formation of white crystals resulting from penetration of moisture through paint-coated walls – especially brick, tile or uncoated plaster. Also produced by soluble materials present in the wall itself.

Emulsifier A substance which acts as a catalyst combining oil, water and varnish into media for painting.

Enamel Made from silicate, enamel pigments are applied to metal plates by various techniques, and fused by firing at high temperatures.

Encaustic Technique of painting either by burning in colour, such as clay into brick, or by the use of hot wax as a medium.

Etching Using acid to incise a metal plate.

Extender, Extending Material used to increase bulk of pigment: the act of adding such material. Often used in cheaper quality paints. Filler, filling, has the same meaning.

F

Fat (adj) Possessing, as in paints, a high proportion of oil.

Ferrule The metal hair or bristle holder of a brush.

Figurative Literally, containing figures. Used loosely to describe non-abstract painting.

Filbert A conical-shaped brush.

Filler See Extender.

Fixatives Thin varnishes, natural or synthetic, sprayed on drawing media for protection.

Flat A flat-shaped brush.

Fugitive Applied to dyes or paints which are short-lived in colour or intensity, due to inherent defects or the action of natural forces, especially sunlight.

G

Gilding Technique of applying gold/silver or gold leaf to a surface, as for frame decoration, for parts of a painting, or in illuminated manuscripts.

Glair Tempera medium made from white of eggs.

Glaze A transparent film of pigment overlying a lighter surface. See, by contrast, Scumble.

Graffito Method in which a line is produced by scratching through one pigmented surface to reveal another.

Graphite A form of carbon. Compressed with fine clay, it is used in the manufacture of pencils.

Grisaille A grey under-painting, laid for subsequent colour glazing.

Grout A mortar used to fill gaps between tiles, etc.

Gum arabic or Gum acacia Hardened sap secreted by acacia trees. Used as a binder for water-soluble pigments.

H

Hatching Graphic technique employing sets of parallel lines to create effect of density or solidity.

Hiding The hiding power of a pigment refers to its opacity.

I

Impasto The thick application of paint or pastel on a surface.

India ink, Indian ink Also Chinese Ink. A dense black ink made from carbon.

Iron oxide Compound from which, in natural or artificial form, many permanent pigments in the yellow and red range are made. See Mars pigments.

J

Japanned Lacquered with a hard resinous varnish.

K

Key (i) In mural painting, the firm wall surface to which paint will adhere without causing crumbling. (ii) Name sometimes given to wedges for canvas stretchers.

Kolinsky Fur of the Siberian mink, hairs from which are used for the finest 'sable' brushes.

L

Lapis lazuli A blue stone from which natural ultramarine pigment is ground. Once widely used, it is now extremely expensive.

Lean (adj) Of paint, possessing little oil in relation to pigment.

Levigation Reduction of material to fine smooth paste or powder.

Lightfastness Ability to resist fading on long exposure to sunlight. Denotes permanence when applied to pigment.

Local colour The inherent or self-contained colour hue of an object or a surface, without modification by light qualities, atmosphere or proximate contrasting colours. Thus the characteristic local colour of a lemon is yellow.

M

Mars pigments Artificial iron oxide pigments, yielding strong tints from yellow through brown to violet.

Mastic Gum or resin obtained from certain coniferous trees, used in varnish, employed as a medium and as a picture protecting surface.

Medium (i) Substance mixed with pigment to form paint, such as oil for oil paints and gum arabic for water colours.
(ii) In oil painting, mixtures of turpentine, oil, varnish, wax etc. which are added to paint to facilitate its application to the support.

Megilp Mixture of linseed oil and mastic (or turpentine) used as a medium.

Mica Aluminium and other silicate minerals. Found usually in granite, either in scales or crystals.

Mottling Appearance of spots or blotches of colour in paint, and on paper.

Mucilage Gum or any viscous substance, derived from plants.

N

Nocturne Painting, usually landscape, made at night.

O

Ochres Natural earths used to make pigments.

Opacity The power of a pigment to cover or obscure the surface to which it is applied.

P

Palette Slab for mixing colours; can be wood, metal, glass, china, marble, perspex or paper. Also denotes range of colours at artist's disposal.

Pigment Colouring-matter made either from natural substances, or synthetically, used in paints and dyes.

Plein-air Painting out of doors.

Polymerization Process of molecular change by which acrylic and other synthetic resins are produced, and by which linseed oil is turned into stand oil.

Polymer paints Paints based on acrylic, or other synthetic, resin.

Polyvinyl acetate A synthetic resin used as a medium or varnish.

Porosity Capacity of material, such as brick or plaster, to absorb moisture through minute surface openings.

Q

Quill In drawing and calligraphy, a pen made from a goose's feather.

R

Rabbit skin From which the best quality of glue size is made.

Rebate In framing, step-shaped cut in reverse side of moulding to receive edge of canvas, board etc.

Relief In printing, a raised surface which receives ink.

Resins Substances obtained from coniferous trees, variously used in media and as varnishes. Synthetic resins are now made by polymerization.

Retouching varnish A weak temporary varnish for oil paintings.

Rouge paper Red paper, similar to carbon paper. Used for transferring drawings, the red marks are easily removed.

S

Sable Animal whose hair is used for making fine soft brushes. See Kolinsky.

Sanguine A red chalk drawing medium.

Saponify Turn into soap by decomposition with alkali.

Scumble To apply a thin, often broken, layer of paint over a darker layer, so modifying the underlying paint. A technique developed by the Venetian School. See, by contrast, Glaze.

Shellac Resinous substance secreted by the lac-insect. It is melted into plates and used in the preparation of varnish.

Silicon Common element, whose compounds – sand, quartz (silica), clay, asbestos and glass – possess inert properties, making them highly suitable for inclusion in a painting medium.

Silverpoint A drawing point made of silver, which is used on a gesso-coated surface.

Size Gelatinous solution, such as rabbit skin glue, used to prepare surface of support for priming and painting.

Stipple Drawing or engraving method employing series of dots rather than lines.

Stylus A pointed instrument used to grave into a softer surface.

Swatch Manufacturer's sample of range of cloths, fabrics or paper.

T

Tempera, Temper Painting processes or media involving an emulsion of oil and water. Normally refers to an egg emulsion.

Tenebroso Style of painting relying on marked contrast between light and shade.

Terra In painting, earth from which pigment can be made, as in Terra vert (Terre verte).

Thixotropic The capacity of fluids to decrease in stiffness when stirred. Such fluids are produced as oil painting media and are included in oil primers. They tend to be fast-drying.

Titanium An oxide used as a white pigment of great permanency and covering powder. Usually extended with other whites to improve its brushing and drying properties.

Tooth Degree of roughness or coarseness in texture of paper or canvas allowing paint film to grip surface.

Torchon or Tortillon A rolled paper stump, or stomp, used for drawing with powdered pigment such as charcoal.

Toxicity Degree or state of poison in a material. Toxic paints include flake white (white lead), whose dry pigment should never be handled, and Naples yellow.

Tragacanth White or reddish gum derived from herbs. Used as a water-soluble binder.

Transfer paper Paper coated with a tint, usually powder, for transferring a drawing to another surface.

U

Ultramarine Blue pigment made from ground lapis lazuli. Rarely used because it is extremely expensive. French ultramarine is an artificial substitute.

V

Value Of colours and tints, the tonal position in the range from white through grey to black.

Vellum Fine parchment, originally calf skin, used traditionally for manuscript.

Venice turpentine Canada balsam, an oil resin or balsam obtained from conifers.

Viscosity The stickiness of fluids; their resistance to flow proportional to pressure applied.

W

Wax Used in painting as a binder. Either beeswax, vegetable wax, or synthetic wax.

Wedges Small, triangular pieces of wood, driven into the interlocking corners of wooden stretchers to produce tension on canvas support. Also called keys.

Whiting Ground and dried chalk used in plate-cleaning and in the preparation of gesso.

Y

Yellowing A tendency on the part of binding media to turn in tint towards yellow. Most likely to occur when linseed oil is included.

Z

Zinc white White formed from zinc oxide, giving pure cool cover. In oil it needs much medium, and has some tendency to crack. In watercolour known as Chinese white.

Zinnober green Another name for Chrome green.

Manufacturers and Suppliers

U.K.

Acorn Art Shop,
28 Colquoun St, Glasgow.

Aitken Dott & Son,
26 Castle St, Edinburgh.

Fred Aldus Ltd.,
37 Lever St, Manchester.

Alexander of Newington,
58 South Clerk St, Edinburgh.

The Arts Centre,
71 Causeyside St, Paisley.

The Arts Centre,
583 Fishponds Rd, Fishponds, Bristol.

Art Repro,
8 De-la-Beche St, Swansea.

The Art Shop,
40 Castle St, Guildford.

The Art Shop,
54 Castle St, Trowbridge.

The Art Shop,
Great Coleman St, Ipswich.

Binney & Smith,
Ampthill Rd, Bedford.

The Blue Gallery,
16 Joy St, Barnstaple.

H. Blyth & Co., 53 Back George St, Manchester.

Brentwood Arts,
106 London Rd, Stockton Heath, Warrington.

Briggs Art & Book Shop,
15 Crouch St, Colchester.

The Chantry Studios,
Pauls Row, High Wycombe.

L. Cornelissen & Son,
22 Great Queen St, Covent Garden, London WC2B 5BH

Cowling & Wilcox,
26 Broadwick St, London W1.

Cumberland
see **Rexel.**

Dahle (UK) Ltd.,
37 Camford Way, Luton, Beds LU3 3AN.

Daler Board Co. Ltd.,
Wareham, Dorset.

J. Davey & Sons Ltd.,
70 Bridge St, Manchester.

The Dollar Gallery,
22 West Burnside, Glasgow.

J. B. Duckett & Co. Ltd.,
74 Bradfield Rd, Sheffield.

The East Anglian Art Shop and Haste Gallery,
3 Great Coleman St, Ipswich.

Falcon Art Supplies Ltd.,
26 George St, Prestwich.

Ivor Fields,
21 Stert St, Abingdon.

W. Frank Gadsby Ltd.,
9 Bradford St, Walsall.

Greyfriars Art Shop,
1 Greyfriars Place, Edinburgh.

Gordons Gallery,
152 Victoria Rd, Scarborough.

Handyman,
43 Tamworth St, Lichfield.

E. Hopper & Co. Ltd.,
48 Market Place, Malton, Yorks.

Langford & Hill,
10 Warwick St, London W1.

Liverpool Fine Arts,
85a Bold St, Liverpool.

Llanelli Art Centre,
31 Market St, Llanelli.

Mair & Son,
46 The Strand, Exmouth.

John Mathieson & Co.,
48 Frederick St, Edinburgh.

A. Perkin & Son,
2a Bletchington Rd, Hove.

Reeves & Sons Ltd.,
Lincoln Rd, Enfield, Middx.

Reeves Art Materials,
178 Kensington High St, London W8.

C. Roberson & Co. Ltd.,
71 Parkway, London NW1.

George Rowney & Co. Ltd.,
P.O. Box 10, Bracknell, Berks.

George Rowney & Co. Ltd.,
121 Percy St, London W1.

Studio 10,
10 Edleston Rd, Crewe.

Torbay Art and Craft Centre,
109 Union St, Torquay.

Trinity Galleries,
Trinity St, Colchester.

Winsor & Newton,
PO Box 91, Wealdstone, Harrow, Middx. HA3 5QN.

U.S.

Alvin & Co. Inc.,
Box 188, Windsor, Conn. 06095; 2418 Teagarden St, San Leandro, Calif. 94577

Arthur Brown & Bro. Inc.,
2 W. 46th St, New York, N.Y. 10036.

Connoisseur Studio,
Box 7187, Louisville, Ky. 40207.

Dahle (USA)
6 Benson Road, Oxford, CT 06483.

Duro Art Supply Co. Inc.,
1832 Juneway Terrace, Chicago, Ill. 60626.

Faber Castell Corp.,
41 Dickerson St, Newark, N.J. 07107.

Gramercy Corp.,
1145 A. W. Custer Place, Denver, Col. 80223.

M. Grumbacher Inc.,
460 West 34th St, New York, N.Y. 10001.

Loew-Correll Inc.,
131 W. Rugby Avenue, Palisades Park, N.J. 07650.

The Morilla Co. Inc.,
43–01 21st St, Long Island City, N.Y. 11101.

Permanent Pigments Inc.,
2700 Highland Avenue, Cincinnati, Ohio 45212.

F. Weber Co.,
Wayne & Windrim Aves, Philadelphia, Pa. 19144.

Winsor & Newton Inc.,
555 Winsor Drive, Secaucus, N.J. 07094.

Yasutomo & Co.,
24 California St, San Francisco, Calif. 94111.

AUSTRALIA

Marcus Art (Australia) Pty Ltd.,
218 Hoddle Street, Abbotsford, Victoria 3067.

J & R Walker (Bemboka),
Bemboka Paper Mill, Bemboka, NSW.

CANADA

Artist Gallery,
3350 Fairview Street, Burlington, Ont. L7N 3L5.

Mona Lisa Art Salon Ltd.,
1518 7th Street, SW Calgary, Alberta T2R 1A7.

Pro-Graphics Ltd.,
6019 4th Street, SE Calgary, Alberta T2H 2A5.

The Art Store,
10054 108th Street, Edmonton, Alberta T5J 3S7.

Rapid Blueprint Inc.,
P.O. Box 306, 35 King William Street, Hamilton, Ont. L8N 3G5.

Hunt Canada International,
5940 Ambler Drive, Mississauga, Ont. L4W 2N3.

Maritime Graphic Arts Limited,
1730 Granville Street, Halifax, Nova Scotia B3J 1X5.

Wallack's Limited,
231 Bank Street, Ottawa, Ont.

Norcal Reprographics Ltd.,
1180 Winnipeg Street, Regina, Saskatchewan S4R 1J6.

M. Francis Kelly Limited,
P.O. Box 5715, 5c Golf Avenue, St. Johns, Newfoundland, A1C 5W8.

Curry's Art Store Limited,
756 Yonge Street, Toronto, Ont. M4Y 2B9.

Loomis & Toles Company Ltd.,
963 Eglington Avenue E., Toronto, Ont. M4G 4B5.

Lynrich Arts Enterprises Ltd.,
64 Gerrard Street E, Toronto, Ont. M5B 1G5.

Selectone Paints Limited,
39 Gail Grove, Toronto, Ont. M9M 1M5.

Hansen's Art Supplies,
1130 Robson Street, Vancouver, B.C. V6E 1B2.

Maxwell Artists Materials Ltd.,
601 West Cordova Street, Vancouver, B.C. V6B 1G1.

Island Blueprint Co. Ltd.,
905F, Fort Street, Victoria, B.C. V8V 3K3.

Fraser Art Supplies Ltd.,
414 Graham Avenue, Winnipeg, Manitoba R3C 0L8.

Lewis Art Supplies,
1438 Erin Street, Winnipeg, Manitoba, R3E 2S8.

Demco Manufacturing Inc.,
1660 Route 209, Franklin Center, Quebec J0S 1E0.

INDEX

Page numbers in *italic* refer to illustrations and captions